AF695299

IMPLEMENTATION OF DUAL CARBON GOALS AND FISCAL SUSTAINABILITY IN THE PEOPLE'S REPUBLIC OF CHINA

JUNE 2026

ASIAN DEVELOPMENT BANK

ADB

6 ADB Avenue, Mandaluyong City, 1550 Metro Manila, Philippines
Tel +63 2 8632 4444; Fax +63 2 8636 2444
www.adb.org

ISBN 978-92-9277-863-7 (print); 978-92-9277-864-4 (PDF); 978-92-9277-865-1 (e-book)
Publication Stock No. TCS260280-2
DOI: http://dx.doi.org/10.22617/TCS260280-2

Notes:
In this publication, "$" refers to United States dollars, "€" refers to European euros, "£" refers to British pounds sterling and "CNY" refers to yuan.

ADB recognizes "China" as the People's Republic of China; "Hong Kong" as Hong Kong, China; "Korea" as the Republic of Korea; "USA" as the United States; and "Macao" as Macau, China..

Prepared by Yongzheng Liu. Remin University of China. For the Government of the People's Republic of China, Ministry of Finance.

Cover design by Ingrid Schroder.

Contents

Tables, Figures, and Boxes

Tables

Figures

Abbreviations

ARIMAX	autoregressive integrated moving average with exogenous variables
CaT	cap and trade
PRC	People's Republic of China
CPC	Communist Party of China
ETS	Emissions Trading System
EU	European Union
GDP	gross domestic product
PPP	public–private partnership
PRCEE	Policy Research Center for Environment and Economy
RGGI	Regional Greenhouse Gas Initiative
UK	United Kingdom
US	United States

Currency Equivalents

Currency unit is CNY
(Chinese renminbi [yuan]).

CNY1.000	=	$0.143
$1.000	=	CNY6.994
€1.000	=	$1.175
$1.000	=	€0.851
£1.000	=	$1.347
$1.000	=	£0.742

Executive Summary

The People's Republic of China (PRC) has committed to peak carbon dioxide emissions before 2030 and achieve carbon neutrality by 2060 (the "dual carbon" goals). Achieving these targets requires a fundamental transformation of the country's energy, industrial, transport, and urban systems. Public finance plays a central role in enabling this transition, yet the associated fiscal costs remain underexplored. This paper systematically reviews the PRC's "1+N" policy framework for carbon peaking and neutrality, assesses existing fiscal and tax instruments, evaluates the short-, medium-, and long-term impacts on fiscal sustainability, and proposes potential public financing tools based on domestic realities and international experience.

The PRC has established a comprehensive policy architecture. The central government's Working Opinions and Action Plan for Carbon Peaking Before 2030 set quantifiable targets for 2025, 2030, and 2060, covering energy efficiency, the share of nonfossil energy, forest coverage, and emissions intensity. These are supported by 10 major actions and provincial implementation plans that tailor national goals to local resource endowments and industrial structures. Fiscal and tax policies rely heavily on direct expenditure measures—special funds, fiscal subsidies, and green public procurement—alongside incentive-based and constraint-based tax policies (e.g., corporate income tax preferences, resource and environmental protection taxes). However, the tax system lacks a dedicated carbon pricing instrument, and market-based financing (green bonds, carbon market, development funds) remains relatively small in scale. This expenditure dominant approach places substantial pressure on fiscal balances.

The paper estimates that achieving the dual carbon goals requires total green investment of CNY100 trillion–CNY200 trillion ("narrow scope") to more than CNY487 trillion ("broad scope") by 2050–2060. Assuming public funds cover about 15% of this need, the annual fiscal investment required is CNY0.5 trillion–CNY2.4 trillion, whereas current energy conservation and environmental protection expenditures average only about CNY0.57 trillion per year, leaving a gap of nearly 1.4% of gross domestic product (GDP). Provincial gaps vary widely, exceeding 8% of GDP in regions like Ningxia and Inner Mongolia. Using a reduced-form ARIMAX model based on provincial carbon peaking targets, the paper finds that an expenditure-driven policy mix would significantly increase government debt and undermine fiscal sustainability. By 2030, the national fiscal revenue–expenditure gap is projected to widen from 5% to 11% of GDP, with even larger deteriorations in coal-dependent and heavy industrial provinces (e.g., Gansu, Inner Mongolia, Liaoning). In contrast, policy combinations that incorporate carbon pricing—such as carbon taxes or auction-based emissions trading—can mitigate fiscal pressures while achieving emissions reductions.

International experience shows that carbon pricing (carbon taxes and emissions trading systems) is the primary public financing tool for climate transition, generating more than $100 billion globally in 2024. The European Union, the United Kingdom, and several states of the United States have successfully used allowance auctions and complementary taxes (e.g., air passenger levies, wealth taxes, carbon border adjustment mechanisms) to raise substantial revenues. Drawing on these lessons, the paper proposes a two-tier strategy for the PRC. In the short term, policy options include (i) shifting from free allowance allocation to paid auctions in the national carbon market, expanding industry coverage, and gradually raising carbon prices; (ii) reducing fossil fuel subsidies and applying differentiated tax relief to high-carbon sectors; and (iii) deepening resource tax reform, raising statutory environmental protection tax rates, and broadening the consumption tax base. In the long term, the PRC should consider introducing a carbon tax (under the environmental protection tax framework, complementing the carbon market), implementing a carbon border adjustment mechanism, levying aviation-related taxes (air passenger tax and aviation fuel tax), exploring a progressive wealth tax, promoting a vehicle miles traveled tax, and prudently advancing a digital services tax.

In conclusion, achieving the dual carbon goals while maintaining fiscal sustainability is feasible, but requires a decisive rebalancing of the policy mix toward revenue-generating instruments. The current expenditure-heavy approach is not sustainable. By developing a multitiered public financing system—combining carbon market auctions, carbon taxes, green tax reforms, and new fiscal tools—the PRC can close the funding gap, reduce fiscal risks, and provide a model for other large emerging economies. Immediate action on short-term measures and systematic planning for long-term instruments are essential to align the country's climate ambitions with sound public finances.

Introduction

Research Background

Since the beginning of the 21st century, global climate change has become increasingly severe. Increased carbon dioxide emissions have led to a chain reaction of rising global temperatures, frequent extreme weather events, and rising sea levels, seriously threatening ecological balance and profoundly impacting the sustainable development of human society. In 2015, at the 21st Conference of the Parties to the United Nations (UN) Framework Convention on Climate Change (COP21), 196 Parties adopted the Paris Agreement, aiming to achieve peak global greenhouse gas emissions as soon as possible and carbon neutrality in the second half of this century through global cooperation.[1] As the world's largest developing country and a major carbon emitter, the carbon emissions strategy of the People's Republic of China (PRC) determines its own sustainable development path and has a profound impact on the global climate governance system. In September 2020, it was announced at the 75th session of the UN General Assembly that "the PRC will increase its nationally determined contributions and adopt more vigorous policies and measures to strive to peak carbon dioxide emissions before 2030 and endeavor to achieve carbon neutrality before 2060 (the 'dual carbon' goals)." Achieving the dual carbon goals is an inevitable requirement for the PRC to build a new development pattern and promote high-quality development, signifying that the PRC's ecological civilization construction has entered a critical period.

Public finance is the foundation and a crucial pillar of national governance, playing an irreplaceable role in achieving the dual carbon goals on schedule. Since 2022, the fiscal authorities have supported the dual carbon goals through public financial support, tax incentives, green government procurement, and diversified investment and financing, providing strong guarantees for pollution reduction and carbon emissions control. At the same time, achieving the dual carbon goals requires a broad and profound systemic transformation of the economy and society, a process that also presents significant challenges to public finance. Supporting the achievement of the dual carbon goals requires substantial fiscal investment. Energy structure transformation, green technology innovation, and improvements to the governance system all require significant infrastructure investment and social capital participation. However, against the backdrop of unprecedented global changes, the PRC's economic development faces the triple pressures of shrinking demand, supply shocks, and weakening expectations. Tax revenue growth is sluggish or even declining, while fiscal expenditure is rigidly increasing due to functions such as improving people's livelihoods, promoting high-quality development and upgrading, and preventing and resolving major risks. Therefore, balancing fiscal revenue and expenditure faces challenges. However, achieving the dual carbon goals means that the transformation based on energy structure transformation will reshape the PRC's economic structure, profoundly affecting the underlying logic and overall pattern of fiscal operations and bringing new challenges. For example,

1 "Carbon peaking" refers to a point in time when carbon dioxide emissions cease to increase and gradually decline after reaching their peak; "carbon neutrality" refers to a point in time when an economy achieves a dynamic balance between carbon removal and emissions through carbon reduction measures.

the energy structure transformation process will lead to a shrinking tax base related to traditional fossil energy, while the time lag and uncertainty of tax contributions from emerging green industries will lead to a fiscal revenue and expenditure gap; the current dual carbon policy system, which focuses on expanding fiscal expenditure but lacks new fiscal financing tools, will also affect the fiscal balance in the future.

Based on this, this research aims to systematically review the PRC's dual carbon goals and their implementation plans at the central, key sectors and industries, and provincial levels. It also aims to systematically summarize the existing fiscal and tax policy tools that support the dual carbon goals, deeply analyze the potential impact of achieving the dual carbon goals on the PRC's fiscal sustainability, and explore potential financing policy tool options to enhance the PRC's fiscal sustainability.

Research Objectives and Methodological Framework

This report aims to achieve the following five objectives through systematic research:

(i) **Institutional framework review.** A comprehensive review of the specific implementation plans for the PRC's dual carbon goals at the central, key sectors and industries, and provincial levels, clarifying the overall plan and specific paths for the PRC to achieve its dual carbon goals.
(ii) **Operational mechanism diagnosis.** Systematic reviews on the current fiscal and tax policies adopted by the PRC to support the implementation of the dual carbon goals and summarize their core characteristics.
(iii) **Core challenges analysis.** This section provides an in-depth analysis of the potential mechanisms by which the dual carbon goals affect fiscal sustainability, and explores the short-term and medium-to-long-term impacts of the dual carbon goals on the PRC's fiscal operations, based on the characteristics of current Chinese fiscal and tax policies.
(iv) **International experience.** Summarize and refine the main financing methods adopted by major countries around the world to achieve green transition, and focus on exploring new policy initiatives in the European Union (EU) and the United States (US) to address the financing needs of carbon neutrality.
(v) **Policy recommendations and design.** Based on the PRC's current institutional realities and international experience, the report proposes potential financing policy tools to enhance the PRC's fiscal sustainability.

Research Content and Structure

This report, following the main thread of "institutional review—challenge analysis—international experience—policy design," constructs a systematic research content and structural framework:

(i) **Introduction.** This section introduces the research background, purpose, and methods, content, and structure of this report.
(ii) **Dual carbon goals and implementation plans of the PRC.** A systematic review of the PRC's central top-level design for dual carbon goals, implementation plans for key areas and industries, and differentiated implementation plans for provinces.

(iii) **Fiscal and tax policy tools supporting the dual carbon goals.** Focusing on three aspects: fiscal expenditure policy, tax policy, and market-oriented and diversified investment policy, this paper systematically reviews the specific fiscal and tax policies adopted by the PRC at present to support the implementation of the dual carbon goals, and extracts the main characteristics of the current policies.

(iv) **The impacts of dual carbon goals on fiscal sustainability.** Focusing on the issue of fiscal sustainability, this paper establishes an analytical framework to analyze the impact of dual carbon goals on fiscal sustainability, and analyzes the potential short-term and medium-to-long-term impacts of dual carbon goals on the PRC's public finances.

(v) **Potential public financing policy tools to enhance fiscal sustainability.** This section summarizes the main financing methods used by major countries worldwide to finance their green transition. It also outlines the policy initiatives of the EU and the US on new fiscal financing methods, considering the additional financing needs of countries achieving carbon neutrality under the Paris Agreement. Based on the PRC's institutional realities and international experience, this section proposes potential short-term and long-term financing policy tools to enhance the PRC's fiscal sustainability.

(vi) **Concluding remarks.** Summarizing the main conclusions of this report and the direction of reform.

Dual Carbon Goals and Implementation Plans of the People's Republic of China

To earnestly fulfill its international commitment to "peak carbon emissions by 2030 and achieve carbon neutrality by 2060," the PRC has taken a holistic and coordinated approach, constructing a comprehensive "1+N" policy framework (Figure 1). This framework integrates measures related to

Figure 1: The People's Republic of China's "1+N" Policy Framework for Carbon Peaking and Carbon Neutrality

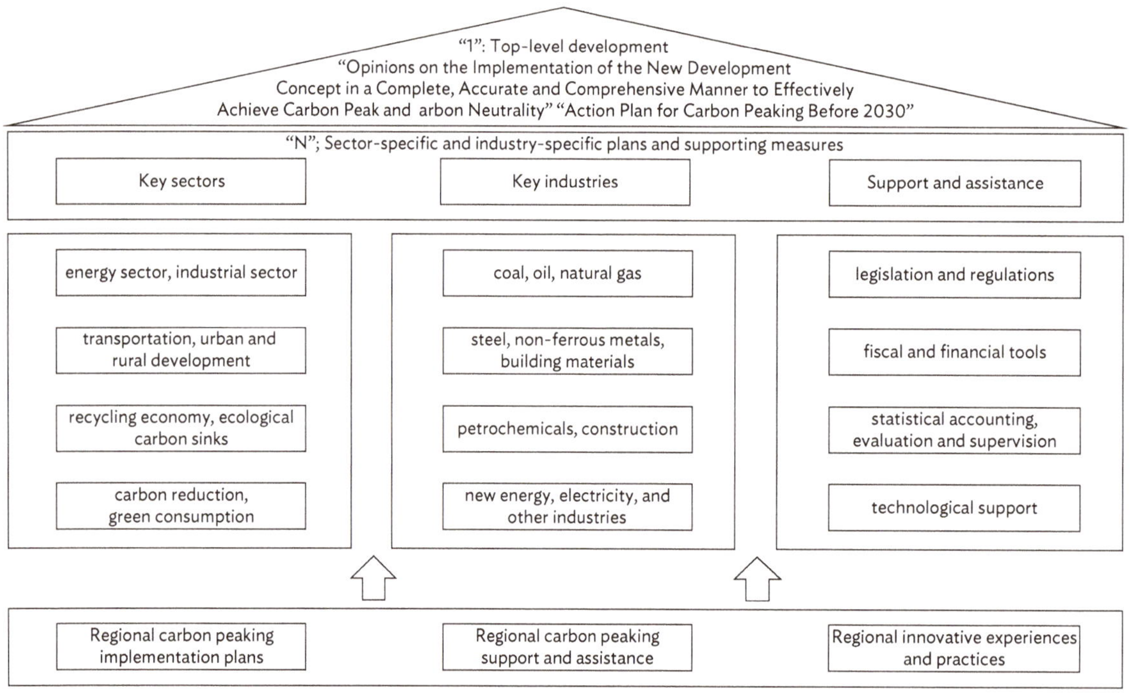

CPC = Communist Party of China.

Note: Referencing Policy Research Center for Environment and Economy (PRCEE) and Environmental Defense Fund (2023). "1" includes the guiding documents issued by the CPC Central Committee and the State Council: Opinions on the Implementation of the New Development Concept in a Complete, Accurate and Comprehensive Manner to Effectively Achieve Carbon Peak and Carbon Neutrality and Action Plan for Carbon Peaking Before 2030; "N" covers special action plans for key areas such as energy, industry, construction, transport, circular economy, technological innovation, carbon sink capacity, public action and regional tiered peaking, as well as key industries such as coal and oil and gas, and supporting policies such as laws and regulations, fiscal policies, financial support, market system, technological innovation, and statistical accounting.

Source: PRCEE and Environmental Defense Fund. 2023. China's Policies and Actions on Carbon Peaking and Carbon Neutrality.

achieving the dual carbon goals into all areas and stages of economic and social development. In this framework, "1" represents the central government's top-level design, guided by the Opinions on the Implementation of the New Development Concept in a Complete, Accurate and Comprehensive Manner to Effectively Achieve Carbon Peak and Carbon Neutrality, and supported by guiding policies such as the Action Plan for Carbon Peaking Before 2030. "N" encompasses specific action plans for key areas and industries, along with a series of supporting safeguard measures. Under the guidance of the 1+N policy framework, all sectors in the PRC are working together to steadily implement the dual carbon goals, promoting the comprehensive sustainable development of the PRC's economy and society.

Central Top-Level Design

The top-level institutional design of the PRC's dual carbon work is based on two major guiding documents: Opinions on the Implementation of the New Development Concept in a Complete, Accurate and Comprehensive Manner to Effectively Achieve Carbon Peak; and Carbon Neutrality and the Action Plan for Carbon Peaking Before 2030. These documents clarify the main objectives, timetable, and road map for achieving dual carbon work and deploy the Ten Major Actions for Carbon Peaking.

(i) Main Objectives and Timeline

The Opinions on the Implementation of the New Development Concept in a Complete, Accurate and Comprehensive Manner to Effectively Achieve Carbon Peak and Carbon Neutrality ("Working Opinions") was jointly issued by the Communist Party of China (CPC) Central Committee and the State Council on 22 September 2021. As the general guideline and blueprint for achieving the dual carbon goals, the Working Opinions elaborates on the overall goals, guiding ideology, working principles, and strategic deployment for promoting dual carbon work, and formulates the main quantitative and qualitative targets for three important time nodes: 2025, 2030, and 2060 (Table 1), providing fundamental guidance for the implementation of dual carbon work. The Working Opinions require:

(a) By 2025, a green, low-carbon, and circular economic system will be established, and energy efficiency in key industries will be significantly improved. Energy consumption per unit of GDP will decrease by 13.5% compared to 2020; carbon dioxide emissions per unit of GDP will decrease by 18% compared to 2020; the proportion of nonfossil energy consumption will reach about 20%; and forest coverage will reach 24.1%, with forest stock reaching 18 billion cubic meters, laying a solid foundation for achieving carbon peaking and carbon neutrality.

(b) By 2030, significant progress will be made in the comprehensive green transformation of economic and social development, with energy efficiency in key energy-consuming industries reaching international advanced levels. Energy consumption per unit of gross domestic product (GDP) will decrease substantially; carbon dioxide emissions per unit of GDP will decrease by more than 65% compared to 2005; the proportion of nonfossil energy consumption will reach about 25%; the total installed capacity of wind and solar power will reach more than 1.2 billion kilowatts; forest coverage will reach about 25%; forest stock will reach 19 billion cubic meters; and carbon dioxide emissions will reach their peak and then steadily decline.

(c) By 2060, a green, low-carbon, and circular economic system and a clean, low-carbon, safe, and efficient energy system will be fully established, energy utilization efficiency will reach international advanced level, the proportion of nonfossil energy consumption will reach more than 80%, the carbon neutrality target will be successfully achieved, fruitful results will be achieved in ecological civilization construction, and a new realm of harmonious coexistence between human and nature will be created.

Table 1: Key Objectives and Timeline for Dual Carbon Goals

Item	2025	2030	2060
Energy utilization rate	Per unit of GDP decreased by 13.5% compared to 2020	per unit of GDP has decreased significantly; the total installed capacity of wind and solar power has reached more than 1.2 billion kilowatts.	Reaching international advanced level
Share of nonfossil energy consumption	20%	25%.	More than 80%
Forest coverage rate	24.1%	25%.	
Forest stock volume	18 billion cubic meters	19 billion cubic meters.	
Carbon dioxide emissions	Emissions per unit of GDP decreased by 18% compared to 2020	Emissions per unit of GDP decreased by more than 65% compared to 2005; emissions peaked and have been steadily declining.	Achieving carbon neutrality

GDP = gross domestic product.

Source: Government of the People's Republic of China. 2021. Opinions on the Implementation of the New Development Concept in a Complete, Accurate and Comprehensive Manner to Effectively Achieve Carbon Peak and Carbon Neutrality.

(ii) Ten Major Actions to Achieve Carbon Peak

In 2021, the State Council issued the Action Plan for Carbon Peaking Before 2030. Following the overall guidance of the Working Opinions, the Action Plan tailors a specific action road map for achieving the key milestone of peaking carbon dioxide emissions by 2030. It breaks down the ambitious goal into quantifiable, assessable, and accountable annual tasks through 10 major actions, providing strong action guarantees for achieving the carbon peaking goals on schedule in 2030.

The Action Plan systematically deploys 10 key actions, including (a) energy green and low-carbon transformation action, building a clean, low-carbon, safe and efficient energy system, and promoting the substitution of non-fossil energy; (b) energy conservation, carbon reduction and efficiency improvement action, comprehensively improving energy utilization efficiency, and promoting energy conservation transformation in key areas; (c) carbon peaking action in the industry sector, promoting the optimization and upgrading of industrial structure, and strengthening energy efficiency constraints in key industries; (d) carbon peaking action in urban and rural construction, developing green and low-carbon buildings, and optimizing the energy consumption structure in urban and rural areas; (e) green and low-carbon action in transportation, optimizing transportation structure, and promoting new energy transportation tools; (f) circular economy to help reduce carbon, building a resource recycling system, and improving resource utilization efficiency; (g) green and low-carbon technological innovation action, breaking through key low-carbon technologies, and promoting the application of green technologies; (h) carbon sink capacity consolidation and improvement action, enhancing the carbon sequestration capacity of the ecosystem, and increasing the incremental amount of ecological carbon sinks; (i) green and low-carbon national action, cultivating green lifestyles, and advocating low-carbon consumption patterns; (j) tiered and orderly carbon peaking action in various regions, formulating peaking plans according to local conditions, and promoting key areas to reach peak first. The specific tasks and objectives—as well as the specific quantitative indicators for the two key assessment milestones of 2025 and 2030—are shown in Table 2.

Table 2: Tasks and Key Indicators of the People's Republic of China's Ten Actions for Carbon Peaking

Number	Action Name	Main Tasks	Key Goals for 2025	Key Goals for 2030
1	Energy Green and Low-Carbon Transition Action	Promote coal consumption substitution and transformation and upgrading; vigorously develop new energy sources; develop hydropower according to local conditions; actively, safely, and orderly develop nuclear power; rationally regulate oil and gas consumption; and accelerate the construction of a new power system.	Strictly and rationally control the growth of coal consumption; ensure that nonfossil energy accounts for more than 20% of total energy consumption; increase hydropower installed capacity by about 40 million kilowatts; and ensure that new energy storage installed capacity reaches more than 30 million kilowatts.	Coal consumption growth will gradually decrease; nonfossil energy will account for more than 25%; newly added hydropower capacity will be about 80 million kilowatts; the total installed capacity of wind power and solar power will reach more than 1.2 billion kilowatts; the installed capacity of pumped storage power stations will reach about 120 million kilowatts; and provincial power grids will have the capacity to respond to peak loads of more than 5%.
2	Energy Conservation, Carbon Reduction and Efficiency Improvement Action	Comprehensively enhance energy conservation management capabilities; implement key energy conservation and carbon reduction projects; promote energy conservation and efficiency improvement of key energy-consuming equipment; and strengthen energy conservation and carbon reduction of new infrastructure.	Per unit of GDP decreased by 13.5% compared to 2020.	Per unit of GDP decreased by more than 65% compared to 2005.

continued on next page

Table 2 *continued*

Number	Action Name	Main Tasks	Key Goals for 2025	Key Goals for 2030
3	Carbon Peak Action in the Industry Sector	Promote green and low-carbon development in the industry sector; promote carbon peaking in the steel, nonferrous metals, building materials, and petrochemical industries; and resolutely curb the blind development of "high energy consumption and high pollution" projects.	Energy efficiency in key industries will reach international advanced levels; domestic crude oil primary processing capacity will be controlled within 1 billion tons; and the capacity utilization rate of major products will be increased to more than 80%.	Accelerate green and low-carbon transformation and high-quality development, and strive to be the first to achieve carbon peaking.
4	Urban and Rural Construction Carbon Peaking Action	Promote the green and low-carbon transformation of urban and rural construction; accelerate the improvement of building energy efficiency; accelerate the optimization of building energy consumption structure; and promote the low-carbon transformation of rural construction and energy consumption.	All new urban buildings will fully implement green building standards; the renewable energy substitution rate of urban buildings will reach 8%; and the rooftop photovoltaic coverage rate of newly built public buildings and new factory buildings will strive to reach 50%.	Building operating energy consumption continues to decline; the renovation rate of buildings in the north has increased significantly.
5	Green and Low-Carbon Actions in Transportation	Promote the low-carbon transformation of transportation vehicles and equipment; build a green and efficient transportation system; and accelerate the construction of green transportation infrastructure.	The proportion of electric vehicles in the public sector has increased significantly; the volume of container rail–water intermodal transport has increased by more than 15% annually.	The proportion of newly added vehicles powered by new energy and clean energy will reach about 40% in the same year; the carbon emissions intensity per unit turnover of operating vehicles will decrease by about 9.5% compared with 2020; the comprehensive energy consumption per unit turnover of national railways will decrease by 10% compared with 2020; the petroleum consumption of land transportation will strive to reach its peak before 2030; the proportion of green travel in cities with a permanent urban population of more than 1 million will not be less than 70%; and the on-site vehicles and equipment of civil transport airports will strive to be fully electrified.

continued on next page

Table 2 *continued*

Number	Action Name	Main Tasks	Key Goals for 2025	Key Goals for 2030
6	Circular Economy Helps Reduce Carbon Emissions	Promote the circular development of industrial parks; strengthen the comprehensive utilization of bulk solid waste; improve the resource recycling system; and vigorously promote the reduction and resource utilization of domestic waste.	Utilization of bulk solid waste will reach about 4 billion tons; the recycling volume of nine major renewable resources—including waste steel, waste copper, waste aluminum, waste lead, waste zinc, waste paper, waste plastic, waste rubber, and waste glass—will reach 450 million tons; and the resource utilization rate of household waste will increase to about 60%.	All key industrial parks at the provincial level and above have implemented circular economy transformation; the annual utilization of solid waste has reached about 4.5 billion tons; the recycling of nine major renewable resources, including scrap steel, has reached 510 million tons; urban household waste classification has achieved full coverage, and the resource utilization rate of household waste has increased to 65%.
7	Green and Low-Carbon Technology Innovation Action	Improve the innovation system and mechanisms; strengthen innovation capacity building and talent cultivation; enhance applied basic research; and accelerate the research, development, and application of advanced and applicable technologies.		Improved institutional mechanisms for scientific and technological innovation, strengthened innovation capabilities, and accelerated green and low-carbon technological revolution.
8	Action to Consolidate and Enhance Carbon Sequestration Capacity	Consolidate the carbon sequestration function of ecosystems; enhance the carbon sink capacity of ecosystems; strengthen the basic support for carbon sinks in ecosystems; and promote emissions reduction and carbon sequestration in agriculture and rural areas.	The national forest coverage rate has reached 24.1%.	The national forest coverage rate has reached 25%; the forest stock volume has reached 19 billion cubic meters.
9	Green and Low-Carbon Action for All	Promote emissions reduction and carbon sequestration in agriculture and rural areas; promote green and low-carbon lifestyles; guide enterprises to fulfill their social responsibilities; and strengthen training for leading cadres.		Enhanced public awareness of conservation, environmental protection, and ecology; advocate a simple, moderate, green, low-carbon, civilized, and healthy lifestyle; and transform green concepts into the conscious actions of all people.

continued on next page

Table 2 *continued*

Number	Action Name	Main Tasks	Key Goals for 2025	Key Goals for 2030
10	Phased and Orderly Carbon Peaking Actions in Various Regions	Scientifically and rationally determine the target for achieving carbon peak; promote green and low-carbon development according to local conditions; formulate local carbon peaking plans through coordinated efforts at all levels; and organize and carry out pilot projects for carbon peaking.		The Beijing–Tianjin–Hebei region, the Yangtze River Delta, and the Guangdong–Hong Kong–Macao Greater Bay Area have taken the lead in promoting a comprehensive green transformation of economic and social development; the Yangtze River Economic Belt, the Yellow River Basin, and national ecological civilization pilot zones are at the forefront of the country in terms of green and low-carbon development; and the central and western regions and the northeastern region are orderly promoting the concentration of high-energy-consuming industries in areas with advantages in clean energy and actively cultivating green development momentum.

GDP = gross domestic product.

Note: The table lists the main tasks and quantitative indicators for each area in the order of action to facilitate horizontal comparison and progress assessment.

Source: Government of the People's Republic of China. 2021. Action Plan for Carbon Peaking Before 2030.

Implementation Plans for Key Areas and Industries

Under the overall leadership of the central government's top-level design, various ministries and commissions have coordinated and focused their efforts, successively formulating specific implementation plans and supporting measures for key areas and industries to achieve the dual carbon goals. This has transformed the top-level design into concrete, actionable measures, ensuring the effective implementation of the dual carbon goals across all sectors and levels. Among the policies represented by "N," key areas include energy, industry, transportation, urban and rural development, agriculture, rural areas, pollution control, and carbon emissions reduction; key industries include coal, oil and gas, steel, non-ferrous metals, petrochemicals, and building materials; and supporting measures include laws and regulations, fiscal policies, financial support, market systems, technological innovation, and statistical accounting.

(i) Energy Sector

As the core source of carbon emissions, the energy sector accounts for more than 80% of the nation's total carbon emissions and shoulders the historical mission of breaking through limitations and transforming the economy.[2] The PRC leads the world in new energy development, but deep-seated contradictions are becoming increasingly apparent: The coal-dominated energy structure has created a high-carbon lock-in, the cost of new energy storage remains high, and there is no opportunity to enhance coordination between standards systems and industrial innovation. The transformation of the energy system, with electricity at its core, is urgently needed.

Since 2021, the National Development and Reform Commission and the National Energy Administration have successively issued a series of guiding policy documents, including the Action Plan for Improving Standardization of Energy Carbon Peaking and Carbon Neutrality, the Implementation Plan for Promoting High-Quality Development of New Energy in the New Era, and the Action Plan for Accelerating the Construction of a New Power System (2024–2027). These documents propose to accelerate the construction of a new power system, enhance the safe and reliable substitution capacity of renewable energy, and promote the formal marketization of new energy grid-connected electricity prices. They also set specific carbon reduction targets and corresponding implementation measures for each stage of the energy sector from 2025 to 2030.

Key objectives. By 2025, the first batch of low-carbon retrofit projects for coal-fired power plants will be fully implemented, achieving a 20% reduction in carbon emissions per kilowatt-hour compared to 2023 through technologies such as biomass co-firing; renewable energy consumption will exceed 1.1 billion tons of standard coal equivalent, with nonfossil energy accounting for 25%; rooftop photovoltaic coverage of newly built public buildings will reach 50%, large-scale wind and solar power bases in deserts and Gobi will be initially established; and an energy standard system will be initially established. By 2027, low-carbon technologies for coal-fired power plants will be mature and widely adopted, with carbon emissions per kilowatt-hour from retrofitted units reduced by 50% compared to 2023, and construction costs reduced by more than 30%; renewable energy supply capacity will be significantly enhanced, and integrated hydropower, wind, and solar power bases will be operational on a large scale; the framework of a new power system will be complete, and the regulation capacity gap will be reduced by 50%. By 2030, renewable energy consumption will reach more than 1.5 billion tons of standard coal equivalent, with nonfossil energy accounting for more than 25%; the total installed capacity of large-scale wind and solar power bases will exceed 500 million kilowatts; coal-fired power plants will be fully transformed into flexible and adjustable power sources; and an energy standard system will fully support the carbon neutrality process.

Key measures. (a) Multidimensional breakthroughs in renewable energy substitution. The government will focus on building a safe and reliable renewable energy supply system; accelerate the construction of large-scale wind and solar power bases in deserts and Gobi, the cluster development of offshore wind power, and the construction of integrated water, wind, and solar power bases; and simultaneously promote the local development of distributed energy and the large-scale development of biomass power generation and solar thermal power generation; strengthen the intelligent upgrading of power grid infrastructure, focus on the development of flexible direct current (DC) transmission and

[2] Government of the People's Republic of China, Belt and Road Energy Cooperation Network. 2023. Developing New Power Systems to Support Dual Carbon Goals.

AC/DC (alternating current-direct current) hybrid distribution network technology, optimize the layout of interprovincial transmission channels, and enhance the renewable energy absorption capacity; and deeply explore the demand-side regulation potential in the fields of industry, construction, and transportation, and guide users to participate in system regulation through the electricity price mechanism.

Guided by the green and low-carbon transformation, the government will promote the deep integration of renewable energy with industries such as industry, transportation, construction, and agriculture, and coordinate efforts in industrial layout, technological transformation, infrastructure construction, and energy structure optimization. In the industry sector, the government will guide the orderly relocation of energy-intensive industries to areas rich in renewable energy, and promote electrified production and low-carbon hydrogen substitution. In the transport sector, the government will accelerate the construction of integrated photovoltaic, energy storage, charging, and discharging facilities, and promote electrification, hydrogen energy, and sustainable fuel applications. In the construction sector, the government will increase the proportion of renewable energy in electricity, heat, and gas, develop near-zero energy and near-zero carbon buildings, and promote clean technologies such as photovoltaics and heat pumps. In the agriculture and rural sector, the government will develop distributed wind and solar power, biomass, and other clean energy sources according to local conditions, improve the heating and energy supply system, and promote electrification and the construction of energy stations. Simultaneously, the government will coordinate the layout of new infrastructure and renewable energy, promote direct green electricity supply and comprehensive energy utilization for, e.g., data centers and 5G base stations, and form a multi-field, multilevel clean energy substitution pattern. Through technological pilot projects and business integration, the government will promote the deep application of renewable energy across multiple fields and industries and cultivate new models and new business formats.

(b) Deepening efforts to reduce carbon emissions in coal-fired power plants. The coal-fired power industry focuses on deep low-carbon upgrades of existing units and on simultaneous construction of low-carbon units. By implementing large-scale biomass co-firing, under the premise of ensuring a long-term stable supply of resources such as agricultural and forestry waste, desert plants, and energy plants, each coal-fired power unit, after renovation, will have the ability to co-fire more than 10% biomass fuel, directly reducing coal consumption and carbon emissions. In parallel, the technology of producing green hydrogen and synthesizing green ammonia from surplus wind and photovoltaic power will be promoted, and green ammonia will be used as a zero-carbon fuel to replace part of the coal. The proportion of green ammonia co-firing in the units will be no less than 10%, and safe ammonia storage facilities will be built outside the plant area to form a new model of coupled power generation of renewable energy, green hydrogen, green ammonia, and coal. On this basis, a high-efficiency carbon capture system such as chemical absorption, adsorption, and membrane separation will be fully equipped to capture carbon dioxide in high purity from coal-fired flue gas for resource utilization scenarios such as oil displacement and production enhancement, hydrogenation to methanol, or injection into geological bodies such as saline aquifers for permanent storage, so as to realize the large-scale consumption and long-term storage of carbon dioxide. The goal is to ensure that by 2027, the carbon emissions per kilowatt-hour of coal-fired power units that have completed low-carbon transformation will be reduced by about 50% compared to the average level of similar units in 2023, with emissions intensity equivalent to that of natural gas power units. This will provide a replicable and scalable demonstration of coal-fired power transformation for building a clean, low-carbon, safe, and efficient new energy system.

(c) Smart upgrading of new power systems. To support the continuous increase in the installed capacity and power generation ratio of new energy sources such as wind power and photovoltaics, efforts should be made to accelerate the construction of a new power system adapted to high proportions of new energy. This requires a comprehensive improvement in the flexible adjustment capability of the power system. The basic platform role of the power grid should be strengthened, the flexible transformation of coal-fired power plants, pumped storage, and solar thermal power generation projects should be vigorously promoted, and the development of new energy storage technologies should be accelerated. At the same time, the potential for demand-side response should be explored in depth to enhance the adjustment capability of the load side. On the other hand, it is necessary to significantly improve the level of distribution network acceptance of distributed new energy sources. This can be achieved by developing distributed smart grids, increasing investment in intelligent transformation, and exploring DC distribution network demonstrations adapted to distributed energy access, to break through the access bottleneck.

Regarding mechanism building, steadily promoting the participation of new energy sources in electricity market transactions is key. This includes supporting direct transactions between new energy projects and users, signing long-term agreements, ensuring the implementation of the full purchase policy, and exploring the contract-for-difference model in the spot market. Simultaneously, it is crucial to further improve the responsibility weighting system for renewable energy power consumption, scientifically set and strictly assess the medium- and long-term consumption targets of various regions, and ensure effective alignment with policies for new renewable energy consumption. These systematic measures collectively constitute important power infrastructure and institutional foundations that support the clean and low-carbon energy transition and ensure the smooth achievement of dual carbon goals.

As a pioneer in energy transition, the State Grid Corporation of the PRC is actively accelerating grid upgrades, building a robust and intelligent grid and energy internet, and supporting the development of distributed energy. It is also vigorously enhancing system regulation capabilities, strengthening the construction and optimized scheduling of regulation resources such as pumped storage, deepening electrification applications, expanding electricity substitution and integrated energy services, and providing comprehensive support for the construction of a new power system and achieving dual carbon goals.

(d) A dual-engine approach of technological breakthroughs and standard guidance. The government will focus on tackling key technologies such as deep-sea floating wind power, large-capacity perovskite tandem photovoltaics, long-term energy storage, green hydrogen production, storage and transportation, fuel cells, co-firing of coal-fired power with biomass and green ammonia, million-ton-level carbon capture and oil recovery, flexible DC transmission, virtual power plants, and coordinated scheduling of power generation, grid, load and storage, to promote the coordinated implementation of multi-energy complementarity and low-carbon transformation of coal-fired power. The government will also gradually improve the full-chain standard system covering nonfossil energy, new power systems, energy storage, hydrogen energy, energy efficiency improvement and carbon emissions reduction, using unified standards to pave the way for the development of clean energy, establish rules for the construction of new power grids, force traditional energy to improve efficiency and transform, and ultimately achieve a green transformation of the entire energy chain.

(ii) Industry Sector

Industry is the largest energy consumer in the PRC. In 2022, the PRC's total energy consumption was 5.41 billion tons of standard coal equivalent, of which industrial consumption accounted for 3.64 billion tons, or 67%. Within the industrial energy consumption structure, manufacturing dominates, with consumption reaching 3.07 billion tons of standard coal equivalent in 2022.[3] Therefore, promoting the green and low-carbon development of industry, especially manufacturing, is the only way to advance the construction of a manufacturing powerhouse and achieve high-quality industrial development, and it is also a key link in achieving the PRC's carbon peaking target.

Based on the Working Opinions and Action Plan, and in conjunction with relevant plans, the Ministry of Industry and Information Technology, the National Development and Reform Commission, and the Ministry of Ecology and Environment jointly issued the Implementation Plan for Carbon Peaking in the Industrial Sector on 1 August 2022. This document details the overall goals for the industry sector and focuses on key industries, developing separate implementation plans and low-carbon development road maps for industries such as steel, building materials, petrochemicals, nonferrous metals, consumer goods, equipment manufacturing, and electronics.

Key objectives. By 2025, energy consumption per unit of added value in industrial enterprises above a designated size will decrease by 13.5% compared to 2020, and the decrease in carbon dioxide emissions per unit of industrial added value will be greater than the overall decrease in society, with a significant reduction in carbon dioxide emissions intensity in key industries. During the 15th 5-year plan period, the industrial structure will be further optimized, industrial energy intensity and carbon dioxide emissions intensity will continue to decline, efforts will be made to reach and reduce carbon peaks, and carbon neutrality capacity will be strengthened on the basis of achieving carbon peaks in the industry sector. A modern industrial system characterized by high efficiency, greenness, circularity, and low carbon will have been established, ensuring that carbon dioxide emissions in the industry sector peak before 2030.

Key measures. Each industry should implement its own policies, promote coordinated progress, and implement the following key actions (Table 3).

3 The data source is the National Bureau of Statistics, and the latest data on total energy consumption by industry is from 2022.

Table 3: Action Plans for Carbon Peaking in Key Industries

Industry	Key Goals for 2025	Key Goals for 2030	Key Tasks and Measures
Steel	Energy consumption per unit product in blast furnace and converter processes will decrease by more than 1% compared to 2023; energy consumption per unit product in electric arc furnace smelting will decrease by more than 2% compared to 2023; comprehensive energy consumption per ton of steel will decrease by more than 2% compared to 2023; the self-generation rate of waste heat, waste pressure and waste energy will increase by more than 3 percentage points compared to 2023; from 2024 to 2025, through the implementation of energy-saving and carbon-reducing transformation and energy-consuming equipment upgrades in the steel industry, energy savings of approximately 20 million tons of standard coal and carbon dioxide emissions reductions of approximately 53 million tons will be achieved.	The energy efficiency of major processes in the steel industry has been further improved; the energy efficiency of major energy-consuming equipment has reached the advanced level; the comprehensive energy consumption and carbon emissions per ton of steel have been significantly reduced; the energy consumption structure has been continuously optimized, and breakthroughs have been made in advanced energy-saving and carbon-reducing technologies such as blast furnace oxygen enrichment technology and hydrogen metallurgy technology; and the industry has achieved remarkable results in green, low-carbon and high-quality development.	Improve capacity regulation and output management; enhance energy conservation and carbon reduction levels in new projects; accelerate energy conservation and carbon reduction transformation and energy equipment upgrades; promote the utilization of waste energy throughout the entire process; increase the proportion of short-process electric arc furnace steelmaking; accelerate the development of new low-carbon smelting models; and improve the level of digital management.
Building Materials	During the 14th 5-year plan period, significant progress was made in the structural adjustment of the building materials industry; energy-saving and low-carbon technologies were continuously promoted in the industry; the unit energy consumption and carbon emissions intensity of key products such as cement, glass, and ceramics continued to decline; and the comprehensive energy consumption level of cement clinker per unit product decreased by more than 3%.	During the 15th 5-year plan period, the industrialization of key green and low-carbon technologies in the building materials industry achieved major breakthroughs; the level of raw material and fuel substitution was greatly improved, and a green, low-carbon, and circular development industrial system was basically established; and the building materials industry ensured to reach carbon peak before 2030.	Strengthen total quantity control; promote raw material substitution; transform energy consumption structure; accelerate technological innovation; and promote green manufacturing.

continued on next page

Table 3 *continued*

Industry	Key Goals for 2025	Key Goals for 2030	Key Tasks and Measures
Petrochemical	Positive progress has been made in "reducing oil and increasing chemicals," with the proportion of refined oil production in newly built integrated refining and chemical projects falling below 40% of crude oil processing volume, and the deployment of large-scale carbon capture, utilization, and storage industrialization demonstration projects being accelerated.	By 2030, short-process synthesis technologies such as one-step synthesis of olefins and ethanol from syngas will be applied on a large scale.	Enhance the supply capacity of raw materials such as natural gas, ethane, and propane. Increase the proportion of low-carbon raw materials; rationally control the scale of coal-to-oil and gas production capacity. Promote the application of raw materials, technologies and equipment for direct oil cracking to produce ethylene and new-generation ion-exchange membrane electrolyzers; and the development of technologies for producing high-value chemicals from renewable energy.
Non-Ferrous Metals	During the 14th 5-year plan period, the industrial structure and energy consumption structure of nonferrous metals will be significantly optimized; the proportion of production capacity above the energy efficiency benchmark level in the electrolytic aluminum industry will reach 30%, and production capacity below the energy efficiency benchmark level will complete technological transformation or be phased out; the utilization rate of renewable energy in the industry will reach more than 25%; the output of recycled aluminum will reach 11.5 million tons; significant progress will be made in the research and application of low-carbon processes; the energy consumption and carbon emissions intensity per unit product of key varieties will be further reduced; and the supply of recycled metals will account for more than 24%.	During the 15th 5-year plan period, the energy consumption structure of the nonferrous metals industry was significantly improved; the proportion of renewable energy used in electrolytic aluminum reached more than 30%; a green, low-carbon, and circular industrial system was established; energy consumption and carbon emissions per unit of product in the electrolytic aluminum industry decreased significantly, the use of renewable energy was further improved, and significant breakthroughs were made in energy-saving and carbon-reducing technologies such as low-temperature aluminum electrolysis, new continuous anode electrolytic cells, inert anode aluminum electrolysis, and graded utilization of recycled aluminum; the supply capacity of high-end aluminum products was greatly improved, and the industry achieved remarkable results in green and low-carbon development; ensuring that the nonferrous metals industry achieves carbon peaking before 2030.	Optimize smelting capacity; adjust and optimize industrial structure; strengthen energy conservation and carbon reduction technologies; promote clean energy substitution; and build a green manufacturing system.

continued on next page

Table 3 *continued*

Industry	Key Goals for 2025	Key Goals for 2030	Key Tasks and Measures
Consumer Goods	Top 30 companies account for 75% of the industry concentration, and the proportion of companies using combined heat and power reaches 85%. The output and proportion of differentiated high-quality green fibers have increased significantly, the application rate of low-temperature and short-process dyeing and printing low-energy consumption technologies has reached 50%, and the proportion of energy recycling technologies has reached 70%.	Cogeneration accounts for more than 90%; the textile industry develops intelligent, efficient, and flexible preparation technologies for chemical fibers, promotes low-energy dyeing and printing equipment, and applies advanced processes such as low-temperature dyeing, low-liquor-ratio dyeing, and continuous dyeing and printing of knitted fabrics; accelerates the recycling of waste textiles; and low-energy dyeing and printing technologies account for 60%.	The paper industry has established a system for the recycling, storage, and transportation of agricultural and forestry biomass residues. Research and develop technologies to replace fossil energy with biomass, and promote low-carbon technologies and equipment such as low-energy cooking, oxygen delignification, wide-pressure zone pressing, and sludge waste heat drying; in the textile industry, develop intelligent, efficient, and flexible chemical fiber preparation technologies, promote low-energy printing and dyeing equipment, and apply low-temperature printing. Advanced technologies such as dyeing, low-liquor-ratio dyeing, and continuous printing and dyeing of knitted fabrics accelerate the recycling of waste textiles.
Equipment Manufacturing	By 2025, advanced near-net-shape forming technologies such as integrated die casting, moldless casting, hot forming of ultra-high strength steel, precision cold forging, welding of dissimilar materials, lightweighting of high-strength alloys, and laser heat treatment will be industrialized.	Innovated and developed a number of advanced green manufacturing technologies to significantly reduce energy consumption in production.	Focusing on the green and low-carbon needs of industries such as power equipment, petrochemical general equipment, heavy machinery, automobiles, ships, and aviation, concentrating on key processes and strengthening the integration of advanced casting, forging, welding, and heat treatment technologies with new technologies. Development should focus on implementing intelligent and green transformation. The promotion of energy-saving and material-saving technologies such as fatigue-resistant manufacturing and lightweight manufacturing should be accelerated; a road map for the green and low-carbon development of power equipment and technologies should be researched and formulated.

continued on next page

Table 3 *continued*

Industry	Key Goals for 2025	Key Goals for 2030	Key Tasks and Measures
Electronic	Continuous crystal pulling technology has applications in more than 95% of industries, while non-electric energy accounts for less than 7% of the lithium battery materials and 2% of the optical fiber industries.	Energy consumption in the manufacturing of electronic materials and electronic products has decreased significantly.	Strengthen industry clustering and low-carbon development, and further reduce the proportion of non-electric energy applications; focusing on electronic materials, components, and typical electronic products, vigorously promote the development of monocrystalline silicon, electrode foil, magnetic materials, lithium battery materials, and electronic ceramics. Improvements in the production processes of electronic glass, optical fibers, and optical fiber preforms; accelerate the promotion of polycrystalline silicon closed-loop manufacturing processes, advanced crystal pulling technology, and energy-saving optical fiber preform and drawing technology. Research and industrial application of clean production technologies for printed circuit boards.

Source: Government of the People's Republic of China. 2022. Implementation Plan for Carbon Peaking in the Industrial Sector. Compiled by the author.

(iii) **Transport Sector**

The transport sector is also a key sector of energy consumption and carbon emissions in the PRC, accounting for about 10% of the country's total carbon emissions, second only to the power and industry sectors.[4] Therefore, emissions reduction in the transport sector has always been one of the country's strategic priorities.

Since 2021, the Ministry of Transport, together with 10 other departments, including the National Development and Reform Commission, has issued the Guiding Opinions on the Integrated Development of Transportation and Energy, and has successively released guiding documents such as the 14th Five-Year Plan for Green Transportation Development. These documents propose accelerating the formation of green and low-carbon transportation modes, strengthening the construction of green infrastructure, promoting new energy, intelligent, digital, and lightweight transportation equipment, and encouraging and guiding green travel, making transportation more environmentally friendly and travel more low-carbon. Under this strategic framework, the PRC is implementing systemic reforms to promote the realization of its dual carbon goals in the transport sector.

4 Central People's Government of the People's Republic of China. 2024. Modern Transportation Moves Towards Intelligent Green Development. 2 September.

Key objectives. By 2025, the average annual growth rate of rail–water intermodal transport volume will exceed 15%, and a green travel network for cities with a population of 1 million will be initially established; the sales share of new energy vehicles will reach 20%; shore power will be fully covered at ports and airports; and charging, battery swapping, and hydrogen refueling networks will be formed. By 2030, land-based oil consumption will be further peaked, and energy consumption per unit turnover of railways will be reduced by 10%, forming a low-carbon travel ecosystem with rail transit as the backbone and slow-moving systems as the network; the proportion of newly added clean-powered vehicles will increase to 40%, the carbon emissions intensity per unit turnover of operating vehicles will decrease by 9.5%, and the green upgrade of inland waterways and the full electrification of airport vehicles will be completed simultaneously, building a clean energy supply system for vehicles and ships.

Key measures. (a) Optimizing the transportation structure and improving transportation organization efficiency. The government will accelerate the construction of a comprehensive three-dimensional transportation network, vigorously develop multimodal transport, promote the construction of dedicated railway lines for industrial and mining enterprises, ports, and logistics parks, accelerate the construction of high-grade inland waterway networks, accelerate the shift of bulk cargo and medium- and long-distance cargo transportation from road to rail and from road to water, and increase the proportion of railways and waterways in comprehensive transportation. The government will also optimize passenger transport organization and guide passenger transport enterprises to operate on a large scale and in an intensive manner; accelerate the construction of urban and rural logistics distribution systems; innovate green, low-carbon, intensive, and efficient distribution models; integrate transportation resources; and improve utilization efficiency.

(b) Promoting the application of new energy sources and driving the low-carbon transformation of transportation vehicles. The government will actively expand the use of new and clean energy sources such as electricity, hydrogen, natural gas, and advanced biofuels in the transport sector. It will vigorously promote new energy vehicles and accelerate their adoption and application in urban public transportation, taxis, logistics and distribution, and other fields, and improve the electrification level of the railway system. The government will accelerate the upgrading and transformation of old ships, actively explore the application of hybrid oil-electric, hydrogen fuel, ammonia fuel, and methanol-powered ships, further promote the use of shore power when ships are docked, and carry out demonstration applications of green and intelligent ships along the coast and inland waterways according to local conditions. The government will also improve the electrification and intelligence of airport operations, develop new energy aircraft, improve the energy efficiency standards of fuel vehicles and ships, improve the energy efficiency labeling system for transportation equipment, and accelerate the elimination of old vehicles and ships with high energy consumption and high emissions.

(c) Accelerating the construction of green transportation infrastructure and actively guiding low-carbon travel. The government will optimize the spatial layout of transport infrastructure and integrate green and low-carbon development into the planning, construction, operation, and maintenance of transportation infrastructure to reduce energy consumption and carbon emissions throughout its entire life cycle. The government will carry out green upgrades and transform transportation infrastructure; further promote the construction of green highways, green ports, and green waterways; and strengthen the construction of urban slow-traffic systems, such as dedicated bicycle lanes and pedestrian walkways. The government will also promote the recycling of transportation resources and will orderly promote the construction of infrastructure such as charging piles, supporting power grids, refueling (gas) stations, and hydrogen refueling stations to improve the level of urban public transportation infrastructure.

(iv) Urban and Rural Construction Sector

The PRC's urbanization process is still in a critical stage of slowing down and improving quality. From 2012 to 2024, the PRC's urbanization rate will increase from 53.1% to 67%, with the urban resident population reaching 944 million and the number of cities nationwide increasing to 694.[5] Carbon emissions from urban and rural construction are expected to continue growing at a relatively significant rate. Against this backdrop, accelerating the green and low-carbon transformation of urban and rural construction and vigorously implementing energy-saving and emission-reduction measures in buildings will have a comprehensive impact on achieving the national dual carbon goals.

Since 2021, the Ministry of Housing and Urban–Rural Development, together with the National Development and Reform Commission and other departments, has issued a series of guiding documents, including the 14th Five-Year Plan for Building Energy Conservation and Green Building Development, the Implementation Plan for Carbon Peaking in Urban and Rural Construction, and the Working Plan for Accelerating Energy Conservation and Carbon Reduction in the Building Sector. These documents systematically outline a green, low-carbon transformation path for urban and rural construction; strive to build a green, low-carbon, and circular development system; and propose specific work objectives and corresponding implementation measures for urban and rural construction.

Key objectives. By 2025, all new urban buildings will fully implement green building standards, prefabricated buildings will account for 30% of all construction, and the renewable energy substitution rate will increase to 8%, laying a solid foundation for carbon peaking. Before 2030, carbon emissions in the urban and rural construction sector will peak, with building electricity accounting for more than 65% of total energy consumption, the electrification of new public buildings reaching 20%, and a green, low-carbon operation model established. Through full-chain emission reduction, efforts will be made to fully build a beautiful living environment where humans and nature coexist harmoniously before 2060.

Key measures. (a) Strengthening building energy conservation and practicing green development. The government will strictly enforce energy efficiency standards for new buildings through a full life cycle management system, clearly require that all new urban buildings fully implement green standards by 2025, and significantly improve the energy efficiency of new residential and public buildings in cold regions by 2030. Buildings are renovated in parallel. In northern regions, energy-saving upgrades for rural houses and urban residences are promoted in close conjunction with clean heating, while public buildings focus on the intelligent adjustment and energy efficiency improvement of key systems such as air-conditioning and lighting, striving to achieve a leap in the overall energy efficiency of electromechanical systems by 2030. The green concept is further penetrated into rural areas. The construction of rural houses actively promotes the application of solar heating and biomass energy technology, and builds a high-standard green building system covering urban and rural areas.

(b) Optimizing the energy structure and promoting clean transformation. The large-scale application of renewable energy is a key priority. The mandatory implementation of rooftop photovoltaic systems for newly built public buildings and factories aims to reach more than half by 2025. At the same

[5] Government of the People's Republic of China, National Development and Reform Commission. 2025. Accurately and Promptly Grasp New Trends in the Urbanization Process and Solidly Promote High-Quality Development of New Urbanization.

time, solar thermal and geothermal energy are promoted in areas with stable hot water demand tailored to local conditions. The deep electrification process of end-use energy is accelerating. Heat pump technology is gradually replacing traditional gas equipment, aiming to significantly increase the proportion of building electricity consumption in energy consumption by 2030. The innovative "photovoltaic-storage–DC-flexible" system integrates photovoltaic power generation, energy storage and distribution, and DC power distribution, promoting buildings to shift from passively consuming energy to actively participating in the energy production and consumption balance.

(c) Innovating construction methods and deepening recycling. The innovation in construction methods is reflected in the vigorous development of prefabricated buildings and the promotion of intelligent construction technology, with the goal of achieving a 40% proportion of prefabricated buildings in new buildings by 2030. The resource recycling closed-loop system is strengthened in tandem, with government projects taking the lead in mandating the purchase of green building materials and setting a goal that star-rated green buildings will fully apply green building materials by 2030; resource consumption and waste generation are strictly controlled during the construction process, with strict upper limits set on the amount of new construction waste emissions, promoting centralized treatment and graded utilization of construction waste, and aiming to achieve a 55% resource utilization rate of construction waste by 2030, striving to achieve a green cycle of the entire life cycle of building materials.

(d) Optimizing urban and rural structure and reshaping spatial pattern. Urban development emphasizes intensive, eco-friendly development, promotes a cluster-style layout, strictly limits the scale of demolition and the width of ecological corridors, and focuses on building convenient 15-minute living circles at the community level. County town construction implements rigid constraints, controls development intensity and building height, and promotes the layout of energy-saving infrastructure. Improving the efficiency of the municipal system is an important support, comprehensively updating old heating pipe networks to reduce heat loss, promoting sponge city construction and reclaimed water utilization throughout the region, significantly increasing the permeable area ratio of built-up areas, and ultimately achieving the synergistic goals of optimizing urban and rural spatial structure, enhancing ecological resilience, and reducing carbon emissions.

(v) Agriculture and Rural Areas

Agriculture and rural areas are only one of the PRC's major sources of carbon emissions, and possess enormous carbon sequestration potential. Promoting emissions reduction and carbon sequestration in agriculture and rural areas, and advancing the green and low-carbon transformation of agriculture, are important aspects of achieving the PRC's dual carbon goals.

Since 2021, the Ministry of Agriculture and Rural Affairs has focused on the dual carbon goals, issuing the 14th Five-Year Plan for National Agricultural Green Development and coordinating it with policies such as the Implementation Plan for Agricultural and Rural Emission Reduction and Carbon Sequestration. It has systematically deployed pathways for agricultural emissions reduction and carbon sequestration, focusing on reducing emissions intensity and enhancing carbon sequestration capacity. Ten major actions have been implemented, including water-saving and methane-reducing measures in crop farming, precision feeding for livestock to reduce emissions, ecological carbon sequestration in fisheries, expanding soil capacity for carbon sequestration in farmland, energy-saving retrofitting of agricultural machinery, and renewable energy substitution. The ministry has also strengthened technological support and the construction of a monitoring system. Furthermore, specific work objectives and implementation measures have been formulated to address issues such as low-carbon transformation, ecological protection, and food security.

Main objectives. By 2025, the PRC will achieve a steady decline in the emissions intensity per unit product of crop farming and animal husbandry, continuously enhance the carbon sequestration capacity of farmland soil, and significantly increase the proportion of clean energy in rural areas; by 2030, the PRC will further reduce the greenhouse gas emissions intensity of agricultural and rural production and life, and make substantial progress in the comprehensive green transformation.

Key measures. (a) Strictly adhering to the bottom line of resource protection and improving utilization efficiency. The government will fully implement the strictest farmland protection system, firmly safeguard the red line of 1.8 billion *mu* of farmland, solidly promote the national black soil protection project, plan to implement 100 million *mu*, and simultaneously promote the comprehensive treatment of 14 million *mu* of degraded farmland.[6] The government will strengthen the rigid constraints on total agricultural water use; vigorously develop efficient dryland agriculture and water-saving irrigation; add 60 million mu of efficient water-saving irrigation area; fully promote water and fertilizer integration technology; improve the farmland irrigation metering facility system; promote the effective utilization coefficient of farmland irrigation water to 0.57; and achieve the goal of saving, intensively utilizing, and efficiently recycling agricultural resources.

(b) Strengthening the fight against pollution and promoting recycling. The government will deepen the implementation of the action to reduce the use of chemical fertilizers and pesticides, increase their efficiency, and strive to achieve a utilization rate of 43% for chemical fertilizers and pesticides for major crops. The government will continue to expand the pilot scope of organic fertilizer substitution for chemical fertilizers, focus on building a whole-chain governance system for agricultural waste, significantly improve the resource utilization rate of livestock and poultry manure to 80%, the comprehensive utilization rate of straw to more than 86%, and the recycling rate of agricultural film to 85%. The government will also improve the extended producer responsibility recycling mechanism for pesticide packaging waste, strictly control agricultural non-point source pollution and white pollution, and promote the coordinated development of agricultural production and the ecological environment.

(c) Systematically restoring the agricultural ecology and enhancing carbon sequestration function. The government will coordinate the integrated protection and systematic management of mountains, rivers, forests, fields, lakes, grasslands, and deserts; fully implement conservation tillage across 140 million mu; and improve the crop rotation and fallow system. The government will strengthen law enforcement and supervision of the 10-year fishing ban in the Yangtze River Basin and the protection of aquatic biological resources, and deepen deep-water-saving, water-control, and ecological restoration projects in the Yellow River Basin. The government will also strengthen the ecological construction of high-standard farmland, vigorously promote the scientific return of straw to the field, and green manure planting technology, continuously improve the organic matter content of the soil, effectively enhance the carbon sequestration capacity of farmland soil, and build a solid ecological barrier for the sustainable development of agriculture and rural areas.

[6] A *mu* is a Chinese unit of measurement (1 *mu* = 666.67 square meters).

(d) Accelerating the green transformation of industries and deepening emissions reduction and carbon sequestration. The government will comprehensively promote the improvement of agricultural varieties, quality enhancement, brand building, and standardized production, and accelerate the development of an ecological circular agriculture system. The government will focus on implementing emissions reduction projects in the planting industry, promote low-carbon rice varieties and optimize irrigation technology to reduce methane emissions; the government will promote carbon reduction actions in animal husbandry, improve feeding technology and manure management to reduce methane and nitrous oxide emissions; it will expand the carbon sink function of fisheries, develop ecological models such as integrated rice-fish farming and build national-level marine ranches. The government will also develop renewable energy sources such as biomass and solar energy in line with local conditions, systematically replace fossil energy consumption in rural production and daily life, and provide solid support for achieving the carbon peak and carbon neutrality targets on schedule.

Provincial Implementation Plan

To implement the dual carbon strategic decision of the CPC Central Committee and the State Council, provinces, autonomous regions and municipalities directly under the Central Government, following the deployment of the Working Opinions and the Action Plan, have formulated localized carbon peaking implementation plans based on their own natural resource endowments, industrial structures, development stages and regional key strategies, and put forward realistic and feasible task objectives and corresponding implementation measures (Appendix, Table A1 shows the implementation plan policy documents of each province).

(i) Carbon Peaking Targets for Each Province

In line with the overall goal of achieving carbon peaking by 2030, regions have formulated quantitative development targets for specific tasks, such as optimizing energy structure and improving energy efficiency, including the proportion of nonfossil energy consumption and energy consumption per unit of GDP (Figures 2 and 3). The overall goals of all regions are highly consistent with the national strategy; however, due to objective conditions, there are significant differences in the specific quantitative targets among regions. For example, in terms of the proportion of nonfossil energy consumption, provinces such as Hainan, Qinghai, and Sichuan have set targets significantly higher than the national requirements, while provinces and municipalities such as Hebei, Shanxi, and Tianjin are relatively conservative; in terms of energy consumption per unit of GDP, provinces such as Liaoning and Shandong have set energy consumption reduction targets that are among the highest in the country, while Gansu Province's targets are relatively low.

Figure 2: Targets for the Share of Nonfossil Energy Consumption in Selected Provinces in 2025 and 2030

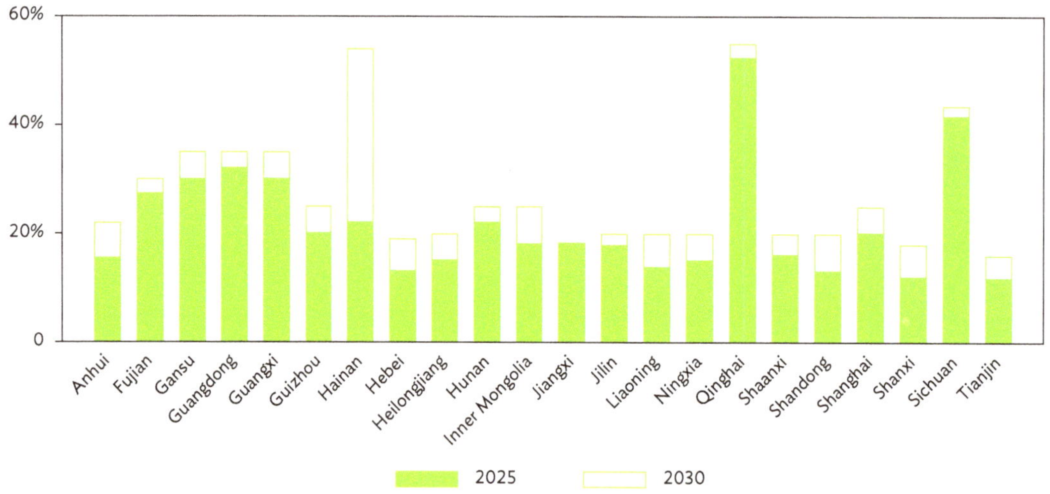

Source: Policy documents on carbon peaking implementation plans of various provinces; compiled by the authors.

Figure 3: Energy Consumption Reduction Targets per Unit of Gross Domestic Product for Some Provinces in 2025 (Compared to 2020)

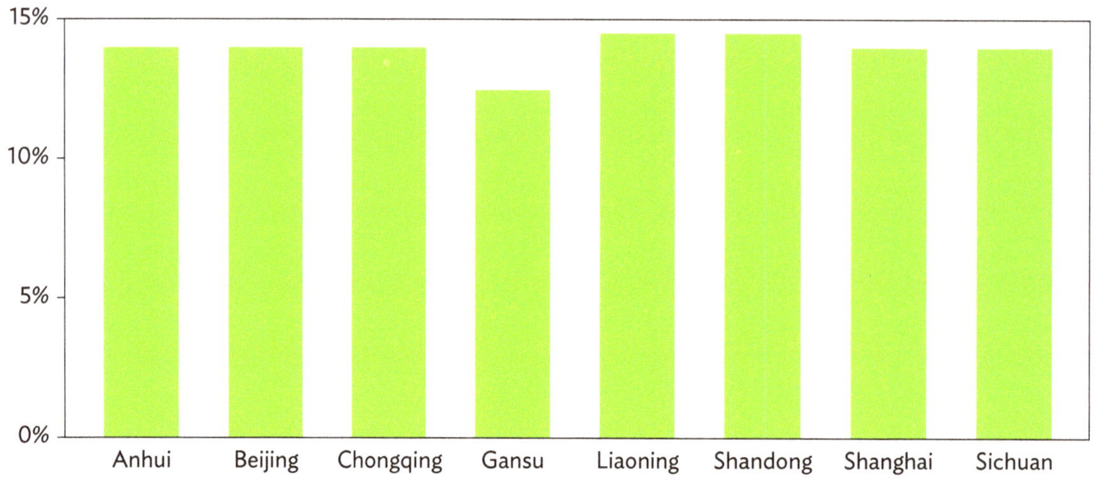

Source: Policy documents on carbon peaking implementation plans of various provinces; compiled by the authors.

(ii) Key Implementation Measures

Based on the specific carbon peaking targets, each province, autonomous region, and municipality has formulated a systematic action plan covering key areas such as energy, industry, transport, and urban and rural construction. In formulating these action plans, each region has proposed consensus-based reform directions, including developing clean energy, improving energy efficiency, promoting the green transformation of key industry sectors, and developing green, low-carbon transportation and green buildings. At the same time, given their resource differences, they have explored and implemented differentiated key measures that reflect local characteristics and strategic priorities, forming a dual carbon working pattern that combines a nationwide approach with localized measures (Table 4).

For example, in the energy sector, the southwestern, northwestern, and eastern coastal provinces are leveraging their abundant local hydropower, wind power, solar power, and tidal power resources to vigorously develop corresponding clean power generation methods, while major coal-fired power provinces such as Shaanxi and Shanxi are focusing on promoting the "three-pronged reform" of coal-fired power generation. In the industry sector, major steel-producing provinces such as Hebei and Jilin are promoting the low-carbon transformation of steelmaking processes, equipment, and technologies, while traditional non-ferrous metal smelting provinces such as Anhui and Shandong are actively promoting the clustered development of the recycled nonferrous metals industry. In the transport sector, coastal and riverine provinces such as Shandong and Tianjin are focusing on building green port demonstration zones; provinces such as Beijing and Jiangsu are emphasizing the construction of intelligent transportation systems; and provinces such as Henan and Sichuan are vigorously developing multimodal transport, including rail-waterway transport. In the urban and rural construction sector, provinces such as Hebei and Shanghai have taken the lead in fully implementing ultra-low energy consumption building standards and improving the green building labeling system; provinces such as Gansu and Shandong are focusing on developing rooftop distributed photovoltaics and promoting green rural housing and energy-saving and environmentally friendly agricultural machinery. In the circular economy sector, provinces such as Shanxi and Tianjin are leveraging their locational advantages and industrial characteristics to explore characteristic resource recycling systems for coastal and resource-based regions, and so on.

Table 4: Key Measures for Carbon Peaking in Various Regions

Key areas	Key initiatives
Energy Sector	• Southwestern provinces such as Guizhou and Sichuan are leveraging their abundant hydropower resources to vigorously develop hydropower and pumped storage, building integrated hydropower, wind power, solar power, thermal power, and energy storage bases, while also considering hydropower development and ecological protection. • Northwestern provinces such as Gansu and Inner Mongolia are leveraging their desert, Gobi, and wasteland resources to build large-scale wind power and photovoltaic bases, focusing on power transmission to other regions and promoting the development of "wind and solar power + energy storage." • Coastal provinces such as Fujian, Guangdong, Hainan, Shandong, and Shanghai are vigorously developing nuclear power and offshore wind power, exploring new marine energy sources such as tidal energy and wave energy, and enhancing regional energy self-sufficiency. • In central and resource-rich provinces such as Anhui, Henan, Jiangxi, Shaanxi, and Shanxi, coal-fired power is the main source of electricity. The focus is on promoting the "three-pronged reform" of coal-fired power (energy conservation and carbon reduction, flexibility, and heating system transformation) to shift coal-fired power from its role as the main source of electricity to a supporting role in peak shaving.

continued on next page

Table 4 *continued*

Key areas	Key initiatives
Industry Sector	• Major steel-producing provinces such as Hebei, Inner Mongolia, and Jilin, as well as other provinces, are strictly promoting capacity replacement and eliminating outdated production capacity, driving the transformation from long-process to short-process steelmaking, vigorously developing electric arc furnace steelmaking, and widely exploring cutting-edge low-carbon technologies such as hydrogen metallurgy, oxygen-enriched smelting, and carbon dioxide capture and utilization. • Anhui, Hebei, and Jiangxi, and other provinces strictly implement capacity replacement and promote the withdrawal of inefficient capacity, implement staggered production of cement on a regular basis, promote the use of bulk solid waste as raw material and clean energy, and accelerate the promotion of low-carbon concrete, new cementitious materials and wood and bamboo building materials, and explore the capture and utilization of carbon in kiln tail gas. • Traditional nonferrous metal smelting provinces and resource-based regions such as Anhui, Gansu, Inner Mongolia, Ningxia, Qinghai, and Shandong are actively promoting the clustered development of the recycled nonferrous metals industry, popularizing low-carbon technologies such as new electrolytic cells, waste heat recovery, and intelligent control, and increasing the proportion of clean energy substitution.
Transport Sector	• Coastal or riverine provinces such as Hebei, Jiangsu, Jiangxi, Shandong, Shanghai, and Tianjin are focusing on promoting full coverage of shore power facilities at ports, upgrading ship power receiving facilities, promoting the application of liquefied natural gas-powered ships and hydrogen fuel cells, and creating green port demonstration zones. • Provinces such as Beijing, Hunan, Jiangsu, and Sichuan are focusing on developing intelligent transportation systems, optimizing the "rail + slow traffic" travel network, improving the efficiency and attractiveness of public transportation through digital means, and systematically guiding citizens to shift toward green travel modes. • Provinces such as Henan, Shandong, Shanxi, and Sichuan are promoting the shift from road to rail and water transport, developing multimodal transport such as rail–waterway, building dedicated railway lines to connect to industrial and mining parks and ports, increasing the proportion of bulk cargo transported by rail, and systematically reducing the carbon emissions intensity of freight transport.
Urban and Rural Construction Sector	• Provinces such as Hebei, Shandong, and Shanghai have taken the lead in fully implementing ultra-low energy consumption building standards and improving the green building labeling system, significantly raising the energy-saving threshold for new buildings and leading the building energy efficiency revolution. • Provinces such as Gansu, Jilin, and Shandong have integrated green and low-carbon development into rural revitalization by promoting rooftop distributed photovoltaics across entire counties, popularizing green farmhouses and energy-saving and environmentally friendly agricultural machinery, and achieving a fundamental transformation in the rural energy consumption structure.
Circular Economy	• Tianjin leverages its coastal location to develop seawater desalination and concentrated brine chemical resource extraction industries, thereby building a distinctive seawater resource recycling system. • In response to the characteristics of its coal-based heavy industry base, Shanxi Province is exploring a green transformation path for resource-based regions by promoting the large-scale application of bulk solid wastes such as coal gangue and fly ash in underground filling and roadbed construction. • Shanghai has taken the lead in achieving the goal of zero landfill of raw household waste by building a comprehensive household waste sorting system and high-standard resource utilization facilities.

Source: Policy documents on carbon peaking implementation plans of various provinces and their compilation by the authors.

Fiscal and Tax Policy Tools Supporting Dual Carbon Goals

Public finance is the foundation and a crucial pillar of national governance, playing a vital role in achieving the dual carbon goals' schedule. As a measure for the Ministry of Finance to implement the Working Opinions and Action Plan, the Ministry of Finance issued the Opinions on Fiscal Support for Achieving Carbon Peaking and Carbon Neutrality in 2022, clarifying six key areas for fiscal support to achieve the dual carbon goals: building a clean, low-carbon safe and efficient energy system; green and low-carbon transformation of key industries; green and low-carbon technological innovation and basic capacity building; green and low-carbon living and resource conservation and utilization; consolidating and enhancing carbon sink capacity; and improving the green and low-carbon market system. Around these areas, **the PRC has gradually established a comprehensive fiscal policy system to promote the green and low-carbon transformation of its economy and society, integrating and utilizing various policy tools, including fiscal expenditure policies, tax policies, and policies guiding diversified market-oriented investment**.

Fiscal Expenditure Policy

Fiscal expenditure policy refers to the government's direct use of fiscal funds to support the green and low-carbon transformation of key areas, thereby promoting the achievement of dual carbon goals. Based on the source and method of use of fiscal funds, fiscal expenditure policy can be further divided into three categories: special funds, fiscal subsidies, and green government procurement.

(i) Special and/or Ad Hoc Funds

To support the dual carbon goals, the central government has established **a series of dedicated funds within its budget to support specific areas, including subsidies for energy conservation and emissions reduction, special funds for energy conservation and carbon reduction, special funds for clean energy development, funds for air pollution prevention and control, and funds for key ecological protection, restoration, and governance**. These special funds vary in scale and purpose, for example:

(a) Energy conservation and emissions reduction subsidies are used to subsidize the new energy vehicle industry and reward the development of charging infrastructure.[7]

[7] The emissions reduction subsidy fund was established in 2015. In 2023, the Ministry of Finance issued the Notice on Amending the Interim Measures for the Management of Energy Conservation and Emission Reduction Subsidy Funds (Cai Jian [2023] No. 58), which adjusted the implementation period and key support scope of the energy conservation and emissions reduction subsidy fund, and emphasized support for the new energy vehicle-related industries.

(b) Special funds for energy conservation and carbon reduction support fossil energy substitution projects, heating infrastructure upgrades and renovations, and waste recycling projects in national carbon peaking pilot cities.
(c) The Clean Energy Development Special Fund is specifically designed to support the development of renewable energy and clean fossil energy.
(d) One important use of air pollution prevention and control funds is to promote clean heating projects in northern regions during winter, thereby achieving cleaner energy consumption while controlling air pollution and creating synergistic benefits of pollution reduction and carbon reduction.[8]
(e) A series of special funds, such as the key ecological protection, restoration, and governance funds, have promoted environmental protection and ecological restoration, and improved the carbon sequestration capacity of the ecological environment.

When applying for these central government special funds, provinces typically also raise corresponding matching funds and set up key support projects tailored to local conditions. For example, in utilizing key ecological protection, restoration, and governance funds, Guangxi Province allocated CNY8.79 billion during the 14th 5-year plan period to protect and restore important regional ecosystems such as the Lijiang River Basin, key sea areas and islands, wetlands, and national nature reserves, enhancing the carbon sequestration capacity of forest, wetland, and marine ecosystems. Since the 14th Five-Year Plan, Liaoning Province has raised CNY7.15 billion from provincial and higher-level funds to vigorously support key projects such as the Three-North Project and the Green Liaoning Project, further enhancing the ecological barrier function and carbon sequestration capacity of the forestry system.

Given that green technology innovation is a crucial driver of achieving the dual carbon goals, many provinces have established special funds to support green and low-carbon-related technological innovation and tackle key technical challenges. For example, Fujian Province has allocated CNY40 million to focus on supporting new energy and energy-saving technologies and to support the establishment of a number of technological innovation platforms; Hubei Province allocates CNY700 million annually from its provincial special funds for technological innovation to support various market entities in carrying out research and development and commercialization of new materials and technologies such as low-carbon, zero-carbon, and negative-carbon technologies; and Jiangsu Province has established a special fund of CNY3 billion to support related scientific and technological research and development, specifically for carbon peaking and carbon neutrality technological innovation.

(ii) Fiscal Subsidies

In addition to special funds, **the public finance department also comprehensively utilizes other forms of fiscal funds to provide direct subsidies to enterprises and residents**. For example, fiscal funds provide subsidies for renewable energy electricity prices based on the difference between the on-grid electricity price and the benchmark coal-fired electricity price to support the transformation to a clean energy system. Several provinces have introduced subsidy policies for purchasing new energy vehicles; for example, Jiangsu Province provided a subsidy of CNY10,000–CNY15,000 per new energy

8 When the special fund for air pollution prevention and control was first established, it emphasized that its purpose was to support the control of air pollution. After the dual carbon goals were proposed, it emphasized supporting air pollution prevention and control, and coordinated response to climate change, demonstrating its support for the dual carbon goals.

vehicle purchased in 2025; Guangxi Province provided a subsidy of CNY8,000–CNY13,000 per new energy vehicle; and Chongqing Municipality provided a fixed subsidy of CNY15,000 for new energy vehicles purchased in 2025. These subsidy policies encourage residents to transition to a green and low-carbon lifestyle. Interest subsidies for green loans are also an important government subsidy tool. The government uses fiscal funds to cover part or all of the interest on green loans, encouraging commercial banks to develop green loan business and reducing the cost of funds for enterprises. For example, banking institutions in Jiangsu and Sichuan provinces, together with local fiscal risk-sharing funds, jointly share risk exposure and provide low-threshold, low-cost credit support for eligible ecological and environmental protection projects through fiscal interest-subsidized loans and risk compensation and mitigation tools. This important subsidy policy has been adopted by many provinces and cities, and has ultimately driven the green transformation of enterprises (Hong, Lin, and Chen 2023).

(iii) Green Government Procurement

Green government procurement is another important tool for fiscal expenditure policies to support the achievement of dual carbon goals. This policy has three major advantages: (a) it reduces enterprises' green technology research and development costs; (b) it alleviates enterprises' financing pressure; and (c) it plays a leading role in guiding social demand for green products (Ma and He, 2022). The PRC has fully implemented the policy of prioritizing and mandating the procurement of energy-saving and environmentally labeled products. The scale of these mandated products accounts for nearly 85% of the procurement scale of similar products. Furthermore, the PRC is continuously expanding the scope of pilot policies supporting green building materials to improve building quality, increasing the types of green building materials from 75 to 108, leading the green and low-carbon transformation and development of the construction industry.[9] In addition, in 2024, the PRC introduced requirements on the proportion of new energy vehicles in government procurement, leveraging the guiding role of government demand to further promote the development of the new energy vehicle industry and guide the green and low-carbon transformation of the automotive industry.

Tax Policy

From a tax policy perspective, the government can change market prices by increasing or decreasing taxes, thereby incentivizing or inhibiting specific behaviors of market entities. Accordingly, tax policies promoting the green and low-carbon transformation of the economy and society can be divided into incentive-based and constraint-based policies. The core purpose of incentive-based tax policies is to provide tax benefits for green and low-carbon activities by enterprises and residents, thereby lowering the cost of such activities and encouraging the low-carbon transition of the economy and society. By contrast, constraint-based tax policies raise the cost of carbon emissions and pollutant discharges for enterprises and residents, thereby discouraging these activities and accelerating energy conservation and emissions reduction. **In the PRC's current tax policies, there are policies directly related to carbon emissions and those centered on environmental pollution. These policies all promote achieving dual carbon goals by incentivizing or inhibiting specific behaviors of market entities**.

[9] Government of the People's Republic of China, Ministry of Finance. 2024. *Report on the Implementation of the PRC's Fiscal Policy in 2024*.

(i) Incentive-Based Tax Policies

Incentive-based tax policies can be divided into three categories:

(a) (a) **Encouraging improved resource utilization efficiency and incentivizing the application of energy-saving and efficient technologies**. For example, the corporate income tax policy provides preferential tax reductions and exemptions (a 3-year exemption and a 3-year half-reduction policy) for enterprises that meet environmental protection, energy-saving, and water-saving requirements; a certain percentage of the energy-saving, water-saving, and environmental protection-related equipment purchased by enterprises can be deducted from the enterprise's tax payable for the year.

(b) (b) **Encouraging residents and enterprises to replace fossil fuels and promoting a cleaner energy consumption system**. Tax policies provide tax incentives for many renewable energy power generation projects, such as the immediate refund of value-added tax for wind power generation and the exemption of urban land use tax for nuclear power plant land, which greatly promotes the development of clean electricity. However, a series of tax incentives for the new energy vehicle industry has been implemented, including reductions and exemptions on purchase tax and vehicle and vessel tax, as well as corporate income tax incentives for high-tech enterprises. These policies promote the clean transformation of energy consumption at the end-user level.

(c) (c) **Encouraging enterprises to develop and apply carbon sequestration technologies to enhance carbon sink capacity**. In addition to encouraging businesses to reduce carbon emissions, tax policies also incentivize them to enhance their carbon emissions management capabilities. For example, eligible carbon capture, utilization, and storage projects can enjoy a 3-year tax exemption and a 3-year tax reduction of half the corporate income tax, and projects that provide protection for plants can enjoy a value-added tax exemption. These tax policies promote improvements in carbon sequestration capacity and are also an important force in driving low-carbon and green transformation.

(ii) Constraint-Based Tax Policies

Constraint-based tax policies primarily focus on two aspects. (a) **Increasing usage costs to incentivize residents and businesses to reduce their use of fossil fuels**. For example, to promote the reduction of fossil fuel consumption, the tax system levies resource taxes on major fossil fuels such as coal, oil, and natural gas, and consumption taxes on finished products such as oil and diesel, thereby increasing the carbon emissions costs for residents and businesses. In addition, by levying environmental protection taxes, the increased cost of emitting pollutants indirectly raises the cost of using fossil fuels for business, thus promoting the green transformation of energy consumption. (b) **Increasing usage costs to strengthen the protection of the ecological carbon sink capacity**. For example, the consumption tax policy includes wooden consumer goods such as disposable wooden chopsticks and solid wood flooring in its tax scope, incentivizing the protection of forest resources; and levies environmental protection taxes on water pollutants containing heavy metals such as mercury and chromium, to incentivize businesses to improve wastewater treatment capabilities, prevent damage to important ecological environments such as lakes and wetlands, and ensure ecological carbon sink capacity.

Table 5 summarizes the main measures of incentive-based and constraint-based tax policies.

Table 5: Summary of Major Tax Policies and Measures

Policy Type	Tax Instrument	Policy Measures
Incentive-Based Tax Policies	Corporate income tax	• Enterprises that meet environmental protection, energy conservation, and water conservation requirements enjoy the "3-year exemption and 3-year half-reduction" policy. • Investment in environmental protection and water-saving equipment can be used to offset tax payable. • High-tech enterprise income tax incentives.
	Value-added tax	• Products and services derived from comprehensive resource utilization are eligible for an immediate tax refund. • Wind power generation enjoys an immediate tax refund. • Heating companies are exempt from value-added tax on heating fees received from individual residents.
	Consumption tax	• Energy-saving and environmentally friendly batteries and coatings are exempt from consumption tax. • The production of pure biodiesel from waste animal and vegetable oils is exempt from consumption tax. • Industrial oils produced from waste mineral oil are exempt from consumption tax.
	Land use tax	• Land used by heating companies that provide heating to residents is exempt from urban land use tax. • The land used for hydropower stations is exempt from urban land use tax. • The land used for nuclear power plants is exempt from urban land use tax.
	Purchase tax and vehicle and vessel tax	• New energy vehicles and vessels are exempt from purchase tax and vehicle and vessel tax.
Constraint-Based Tax Policies	Resource tax	• Resource tax levied on fossil fuels such as coal, oil, and natural gas. • Resource tax levied on water resources.
	Environmental protection tax	• Taxation of air pollutants such as sulfur dioxide and nitrogen oxides. • Taxation on water pollutants containing heavy metals such as mercury and chromium.
	Consumption tax	• Taxation on refined oil products, including gasoline and diesel. • Taxation on wooden disposable chopsticks, solid wood flooring, and other wood products.

Source: Compiled by the author.

Market-Oriented and Diversified Investment Policies

Achieving the dual carbon goals requires a green transformation of the entire economy and society, which demands investment far beyond the scale that fiscal funds can support. Therefore, fiscal funds must play a leading role in attracting social capital to actively participate in the green transformation. The PRC has initially established a diversified funding system to attract social capital participation, including green development funds, green government bonds, and carbon emissions trading markets.

(i) Green Development Fund

Green development funds are typically government-funded and attract diverse capital, including banks and private capital, to support green industries and the green transformation of key industries. In 2020, the Ministry of Finance led the establishment of the National Green Development Fund in Shanghai, with a total scale of CNY88.5 billion. This fund employs three investment methods: project investment, equity investment, and sub-fund investment, focusing on green development areas such as environmental protection and pollution prevention, ecological restoration and land greening, and energy and resource conservation. In 2023, the National Green Development Fund approved investments in 26 projects, totaling CNY12.69 billion. Approximately 72% of the investment was in ecological and environmental protection, and more than 12,000 *mu* of ecological restoration area was completed, achieving significant environmental and social benefits.[10]

Many provinces and cities have also utilized green development funds as an important tool, combining fiscal funds and private capital to establish green industry investment funds. These funds tailor investment areas and projects to local conditions, promoting faster green transformation of the local economy. For example, in 2023, Panzhihua City raised CNY3 billion to establish a green and low-carbon industry fund, focusing on investments in strategic, emerging, and high-growth industries such as new energy, new materials, modern manufacturing, and cultural tourism, to support the integration and improvement of the industrial chain. In addition, local governments are actively introducing international green development funds, leveraging their geographic advantages to expand fundraising channels. For instance, the Weihai Municipal Government, in conjunction with the UN Green Climate Fund, established the Shandong Green Development Fund Weihai Parallel Fund, with a total scale of CNY1 billion and an initial phase of CNY500 million, providing impetus for Shandong Province to deepen the transformation of old and new growth drivers. Appendix, Table A2 lists practical cases from other provinces and cities.

As an important component of the normalized government fiscal investment mechanism and the green finance system, the Green Development Fund, funded by fiscal resources, has fully leveraged its multiplier effect, attracting large-scale social capital investment in key areas of dual carbon and creating significant benefits.

(ii) Green Government Bonds

As an effective fiscal tool, green government bonds play a crucial role in ensuring the supply of green public goods, guiding industrial restructuring and upgrading, and stimulating private capital investment in green sectors. Green government bonds are used for green projects, with dedicated accounts or ledgers established to regularly disclose fund usage and environmental benefits. In 2015, the PRC clarified the top-level design for establishing a green finance system, and the central and local governments introduced numerous regulations and incentive policies, putting green government bonds into practice. At the local level, cities in the eastern and central regions of the PRC have widely experimented with issuing green bonds with carbon revenue, green project revenue, and green asset qualifications as core elements, raising funds domestically and internationally to support the development of dual carbon projects. For example, Jiangxi issued green municipal special bonds in 2019, Guangdong issued water resource special bonds in 2020, and Hainan Province issued offshore government special bonds for marine economy, marine protection, and green environmental protection projects in 2022. These bonds are mainly invested in areas such as sustainable water resources and wastewater management, pollution prevention and control, ecological environment governance, clean energy, and clean transportation. The funds are included in government budget management and listed under the relevant budget items, providing a feasible solution to address the funding gap required to achieve the dual carbon goals.

10 Source: National Green Development Fund. 2024. National Green Development Fund ESG Report (2023)..

(iii) Carbon Emissions Trading Market

The carbon emissions trading market is a market mechanism designed to achieve greenhouse gas emissions reduction targets based on the principles of cap-and-trade. Its core content involves the government setting a cap on total carbon emissions and allowing companies to trade carbon emissions allowances within this cap, thereby achieving emissions reduction targets in the most cost-effective way. Since 2013, the PRC has conducted carbon emissions trading pilot programs in seven provinces and municipalities, including Beijing, Chongqing, Guangdong, Hubei, Shanghai, Shenzhen, and Tianjin. These pilot provinces and municipalities, based on the establishment of trading platforms and verification systems, prioritized special fiscal funds to support emitting entities that actively participated in trading and fulfilled their obligations, accumulating experience for a unified national carbon market. In 2021, the national carbon emissions trading market officially launched. Through the trading of carbon emissions allowances and other spot products, it monitors the carbon emissions information of key emitting entities, imposes costs on companies' carbon emissions behavior, and accelerates their green transformation. In addition, the government also encourages companies to use carbon allowances as collateral for loans to improve their financing conditions, increase market liquidity, and guide more market funds into important areas of green and low-carbon transformation.[11] As of July 2025, the national carbon market had accumulated a total trading volume of 672 million tons, with a total transaction value exceeding CNY46.1 billion. At the local level, many provinces have also emphasized the importance of developing carbon emissions trading markets and formulated their own specific measures. For example, Guangdong, for the first time at the provincial level, explicitly stated that carbon emissions allowances are legal collateral; Guizhou launched a "forestry carbon ticket" credit enhancement model and created "carbon reduction loans." The continuous improvement of the carbon emissions trading market helps to leverage the synergistic effect of the fiscal and financial systems, promote diversified financing in key areas of the dual carbon goals, and drive the green transformation of the economy and society.

Main Characteristics of Current Policies

In summary, the PRC has gradually established a complete fiscal and tax policy system to support the achievement of its dual carbon goals, and it exhibits the following main characteristics:

(i) Fiscal Expenditure Policy Plays a Dominant Role

Since the release of the Working Opinions and Action Plan in 2021, the Ministry of Finance has successively established a series of special funds to promote the achievement of dual carbon goals, including those for energy conservation and carbon reduction, energy conservation and emissions reduction, and clean energy development. These funds support the construction of a clean, low-carbon, and efficient energy system and the low-carbon transformation of key areas and industries. In terms of the scale of fiscal expenditure, **during 2020–2024, the central government invested approximately CNY500 million–CNY600 billion annually in ecological protection and green development support** (Liao, 2024). In 2024 alone, the central government allocated more than CNY25 billion to promote the new energy vehicle industry, CNY34 billion to air pollution prevention

[11] X. Pang. 2024. Functional Analysis, Progress and Policy Recommendations of The PRC's Carbon Finance Market. International Institute of Green Finance, Central University of Finance and Economics.

and control, and more than CNY4.6 billion to clean energy development.[12] In terms of institutional guarantees, the Ministry of Finance has successively issued documents to ensure that special funds are used for dual carbon projects through measures such as improving fund management methods and process reengineering. For example, in 2023, the Ministry of Finance issued the Notice on Amending the Interim Measures for the Management of Energy Conservation and Emission Reduction Subsidies, revising the scope of use of fiscal support funds for energy conservation and emissions reduction, and clarifying support for six aspects, including the promotion and application of new energy vehicles, charging pile infrastructure, and the demonstration application of fuel cell vehicles. In 2024, the Ministry of Finance revised the Measures for the Management of Key Ecological Protection, Restoration and Governance Funds, emphasizing that governance funds should primarily support integrated protection and restoration projects of mountains, rivers, forests, fields, lakes, grasslands, and deserts, as well as the remediation of historically abandoned industrial and mining land, explicitly stating that funds should be prioritized for addressing prominent ecological and environmental issues. Furthermore, to improve the efficiency of central government fund utilization and mobilize social capital to participate in energy conservation and carbon reduction, the National Development and Reform Commission issued the Measures for the Special Management of Central Budgetary Investment in Energy Conservation and Carbon Reduction in 2024, explicitly emphasizing that a portion of the central budgetary investment funds should be used specifically to support energy conservation and carbon reduction in key industries and key areas, and to promote carbon reduction through the circular economy.

(ii) Tax Policies Lack Tools That Consider Financing for the Dual Carbon Goals

Tax policies have constructed a series of policy combinations conducive to achieving dual carbon goals from both incentive and constraint perspectives. Among them, **tax incentive policies aimed at incentivizing enterprises have played a key guiding role in promoting green development and transformation**. For example, Shenzhen reduced or exempted CNY14.52 billion in purchase tax and CNY578 million in vehicle and vessel tax for new energy vehicles between 2020 and 2022, promoting the popularization of new energy vehicles and driving Shenzhen's new energy vehicle industry into a new stage of large-scale and rapid development.[13] At the same time, such tax incentive policies have also become a major tool for the finance department to promote dual carbon goals. Specifically, after the dual carbon goals were proposed, the Ministry of Finance made targeted adjustments to the scope of tax incentives for some tax categories. For example, in 2021, the Ministry of Finance issued the Catalog of Enterprise Income Tax Incentives for Environmental Protection, Energy Conservation, and Water Conservation Projects (2021 Edition) and the Catalog of Enterprise Income Tax Incentives for Comprehensive Resource Utilization (2021 Edition), expanding the scope of water-saving, energy-saving, and clean energy technologies and equipment eligible for preferential treatment. Also in 2021, the Ministry of Finance issued the Announcement on Improving the Value-Added Tax (VAT) Policy for Comprehensive Resource Utilization, stipulating that taxpayers engaged in eligible comprehensive resource utilization projects can enjoy immediate VAT refunds. However, it should be noted that the essence of tax incentive policies is tax expenditure. While they promote energy conservation, emissions reduction, and green transformation for enterprises, they also reduce tax revenue, thereby increasing the fiscal burden to some extent.

[12] Central Government to Local Government Transfer Payment Management Platform of the Ministry of Finance. (https://www.mof.gov.cn/zhuantihuigu/cczqzyzfglbf/)

[13] Shenzhen Municipal Development and Reform Commission.

From an international perspective, achieving a green transformation across society requires substantial fiscal investment. A reasonable tax policy should help promote energy conservation and emissions reduction among enterprises and residents, but also consider the government's practical need to secure sufficient fiscal resources to support its dual carbon goals. In this regard, the PRC's green tax system—centered on environmental protection tax and supplemented by resource tax, consumption tax, and other taxes—still has scope for further enhancement. **The green tax system has a narrow scope, and its tax rates are not entirely reasonable**. For example, the current resource tax rate is generally too low and does not consider resource scarcity; the consumption tax has a narrow scope and excludes important fossil fuels such as coal. These problems inhibit the overall regulatory power of the green tax system; if the regulatory power of the green tax system on the green economic transformation is measured by the proportion of green tax revenue to total tax revenue, then the PRC is at the lower end of the levels of the countries of the Organisation for Economic Co-operation and Development (OECD) (Ma and Wang, 2021). **However, the green tax system lacks tax instruments that directly use carbon emissions as a tax base**. Based on the experience of developed countries, establishing a carbon tax has two advantages for achieving the dual carbon goals. (a) A carbon tax directly targets carbon emissions behavior, increasing the cost of carbon emissions and directly incentivizing businesses and households to reduce emissions and carbon footprints, making it highly targeted; and (b) A carbon tax has significant financing potential, capable of bridging the funding gap in achieving dual carbon goals. Research by the Paris Climate Economy Institute shows that in 2024, 43 countries worldwide implemented carbon taxes, raising more than $30 billion; considering that current carbon tax rates are generally low, their financing potential still has considerable room for future expansion.[14]

(iii) Fiscal Funds Are Scattered and Insufficient, and Market-Oriented and Diversified Investment Is Still Small in Scale

According to research estimates, the PRC needs to invest more than CNY100 trillion to achieve its dual carbon goals, with fiscal funds covering 10%–15% of this (Jiang and Chen, 2023). The PRC's expenditure intensity for achieving its dual carbon goals remains relatively low: In 2019, energy conservation and environmental protection expenditures accounted for 0.73% of GDP in national fiscal expenditures, and this figure gradually declined to 0.41% in 2023 (CNY548.9 billion). Furthermore, current fiscal expenditures on dual carbon are scattered across multiple departments, including ecological environment, development and reform, and agriculture and rural affairs. This makes it difficult for funds from various sectors to work synergistically, leading to duplicate support and inefficient use of funds (Zhang, 2022). The main reason behind this is that fiscal support policies for various dual carbon goals are scattered across multiple sectors, such as energy, industry, and transportation, lacking a unified policy approach and objectives, making it difficult to form policy synergy and resulting in low efficiency in the use of funds.[15]

[14] G. Cayol et al. 2025. Global Carbon Accounts 2025: Carbon Pricing Instruments and the Unlocked Potential of Carbon Revenues.

[15] China Finance. 2024. Jiangsu: Implementing the "Dual Carbon" Strategy to Fully Promote Green Development [J]. 2024(23). pp. 28–31.

The funding gap in achieving the dual carbon goals requires more reliance on diversified market-based investment. The PRC has attracted social capital investment through green industry funds, green government bonds, and carbon market trading, but the overall scale remains relatively small. Taking carbon market trading as an example, in 2024, the EU's carbon emissions trading system raised €42 billion, with most of the funds used for climate transition and environmental protection, providing crucial financial support for promoting the green transformation of the economy and society (footnote 14). In contrast, **the PRC's carbon emissions trading market is still in the stage of issuing allowances to enterprises free of charge, and it adopts an intensity-based allowance calculation method, meaning it does not set an absolute total allowance, which effectively limits its ability to finance the government**.

The Impacts of Dual Carbon Goals on Fiscal Sustainability

Basic Analytical Framework

Achieving the dual carbon goals signifies a broad and profound systemic transformation of the economy and society, a process that also has a significant impact on public finance. **A series of policy measures to advance the dual carbon goals can directly or indirectly affect government fiscal revenue and expenditure through various channels in the short, medium, and long term, thereby influencing the fiscal balance.** This section discusses and explains the key transmission channels involved.

In general, the dual carbon policy can affect fiscal balance through both direct and indirect effects (Figure 4). **Direct effects refer to the impact of the policy's implementation on fiscal balance**. For example, the substantial government spending and/or tax incentives required for policy implementation directly affect the current fiscal balance. **Indirect effects refer to the impact of**

Figure 4: Basic Analytical Framework for the Impact of Dual Carbon Policies on Fiscal Sustainability

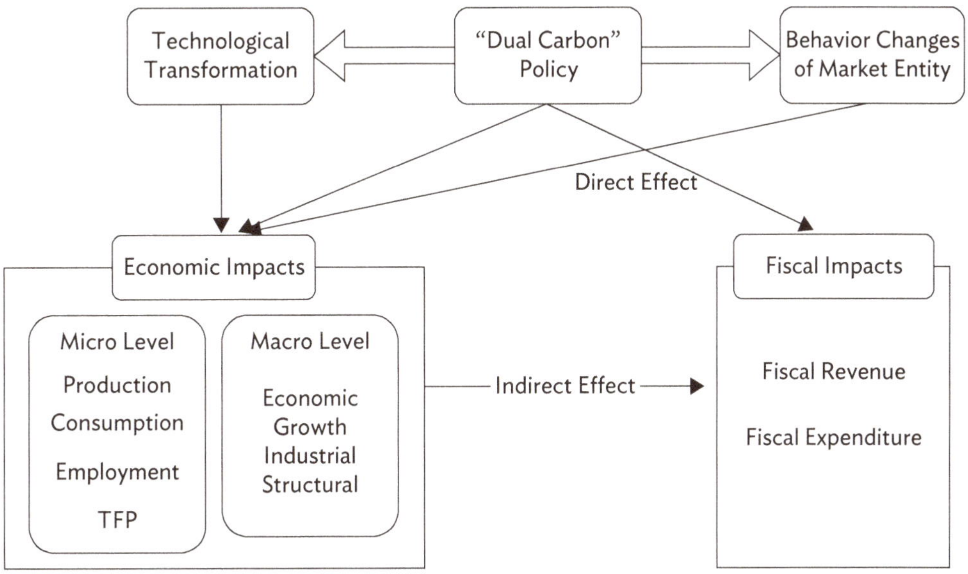

TFP = total factor productivity.
Source: Compiled by the author.

policy implementation on economic activities and, consequently, on government revenue and expenditure, by altering costs and prices or by guiding technological change through subsidy and funding allocations. For example, implementing a carbon trading market increases the unit cost of carbon emissions, inhibits the production of traditional coal- and oil-related products, and, in the long term, affects government tax revenue from fossil fuel products. **In summary, regardless of direct or indirect effects, the dual carbon policies affect fiscal balance through both (short-term or long-term) fiscal revenue and expenditure**.

(i) Mechanism of Impacts

(a) Fiscal Revenue Channel

The impact of the dual carbon policy on fiscal revenue is complex and has both positive and negative effects. Different policy tools operate through different mechanisms, potentially having a positive or negative impact on fiscal revenue growth through direct or indirect effects. Furthermore, these impacts often change dynamically.

By establishing a series of carbon pricing mechanisms, such as carbon taxes and carbon emissions trading systems, or by eliminating tax incentives for fossil fuels, governments can directly and effectively increase short-term fiscal revenue. Taking carbon pricing—a representative core policy tool—as an example, levying a carbon tax can internalize the external costs of carbon emissions, achieving the dual carbon goal at a lower cost, opening new sources of government revenue, and allowing it to obtain additional fiscal revenue. Black et al. (2024) used the climate policy assessment tool (CPAT) to show that carbon taxes can generate additional fiscal revenue for high-, medium-, and low-income countries.[16] In a simulated scenario in which the carbon pricing system is fully market-driven, carbon taxes in high-income countries such as the EU and the US can contribute fiscal revenue equivalent to 0.5%–3.0% of GDP. If the PRC can fully implement a carbon tax (or carbon emissions trading system), it will be able to create fiscal revenue of about 3% of GDP; even if a cap is set on carbon pricing, the PRC's carbon tax system can still create fiscal revenue of more than 1.5% of GDP. Therefore, in the early stages of achieving the dual carbon goals, levying carbon taxes and other measures can create huge "fiscal dividends" for the government. However, as efforts to control carbon emissions continue, the costs for residents and businesses to reduce their carbon footprint are continually rising, and society as a whole is gradually shifting toward green, low-carbon production and lifestyles. **The decline in carbon emissions and the reduction in traditional fossil fuel consumption will lead to a continuous shrinking tax base for carbon taxes and fossil fuel-related taxes, resulting in a gradual decrease in corresponding fiscal revenue. Therefore, in the long run, the fiscal revenue growth brought about by implementing carbon pricing and reducing fossil fuel tax incentives is unsustainable**.

16 The Climate Policy Assessment Tool (CPAT) is a model jointly developed by the International Monetary Fund (IMF) and the World Bank to assess the effectiveness of environmental policies in various countries. This model uses detailed economic data from each country to estimate key characteristic parameters of the economy and can simulate the impact of various policies on macroeconomic variables such as GDP and fiscal revenue.

Government measures to restrict the development of traditional, high-pollution, and energy-intensive enterprises and to support green technology innovation and industrial upgrading will also have an adverse impact on short-term fiscal revenue. Industries such as steel and petrochemicals will be restricted in their development during the transformation, and their tax-generating capacity will continue to decline rapidly. These industries usually occupy a very important position in the national economy and make a significant contribution to fiscal revenue, so industrial transformation will indirectly lead to a fiscal revenue gap in the early and medium term. However, the government will also support the development of emerging green industries, such as new energy vehicles and renewable energy power generation projects. The development cycle of green emerging industries is relatively long, and their growth is often accompanied by the implementation of supporting tax incentives, such as accelerated depreciation and investment tax credits, which may further reduce expected short-term tax revenue. Only when traditional high-energy-consuming industries successfully complete their green transformation, and the fiscal revenue contributed by emerging green industries continues to grow, ultimately forming a new tax structure under the green economy model, will the fiscal revenue of relevant industries gradually recover.

(b) Fiscal Expenditure Channel

For fiscal expenditures, the impact of the dual carbon policy is also multifaceted, yielding different results in the short and long term.

To ensure the timely achievement of the dual carbon goals, the government needs to invest heavily in supporting the transformation of society, businesses, and households toward green and low-carbon practices. This will significantly increase fiscal expenditure pressure in the short term. Specifically, green and low-carbon investment—as well as household subsidies—are two important policy tools the government uses to implement the dual carbon policy. Regarding green and low-carbon investment, the government needs to vigorously promote investment in green infrastructure—such as green smart grids and charging and/or battery-swapping facilities—to improve and upgrade the key infrastructure system. Fiscal funds need to continuously support enterprises undergoing green transformation to incentivize them to improve energy efficiency and achieve emissions reduction, carbon reduction, and green development. Therefore, in the early stages of implementing the dual carbon work, the increase in government green and low-carbon investment expenditure will directly generate significant fiscal expenditure pressure. Meanwhile, household subsidies can be divided into two categories. The first category involves targeted government subsidies for low-income families who may face higher living costs due to the green transition, such as subsidies to offset additional costs incurred by using clean energy. The second category involves subsidies for families facing unemployment or income loss due to economic restructuring caused by dual carbon goals, along with targeted workforce training programs to ensure their standard of living. In the early stages of the green transition, dual carbon policies will gradually increase energy prices, weakening the purchasing power of low-income groups. Furthermore, some energy-intensive industries may shrink or even exit the market due to rising costs and policy constraints, leading to short-term employment pressure. The resulting increase in social security and unemployment relief expenditures will further indirectly exacerbate the fiscal burden (Andersson, Baccianti, and Morgan 2020).

In the long run, as the peak period of green infrastructure construction ends and the green and low-carbon transformation of the socioeconomic system is completed, the pressure on fiscal expenditure caused by investment and household subsidies will tend to ease. A large amount of investment in green infrastructure will shift to maintenance expenditures for various facilities. At the same time, as the clean energy system gradually matures, government subsidies to related industries can be gradually phased out, reducing the government's need for direct investment expenditures. However, socioeconomic development will improve residents' health, which may indirectly reduce social medical security expenditures and improve overall social productivity.

Conversely, eliminating subsidies for fossil fuels could save governments significant fiscal expenditure. Many countries still provide substantial subsidies for the production and consumption of fossil fuels, driven by considerations such as lowering energy prices and promoting industrial development. Indirect subsidies include fossil fuel tax breaks and low-interest loans, while direct subsidies include direct government payments to fossil fuel producers or consumers, price support, and tax rebates. Therefore, reducing or eliminating fossil fuel subsidies could increase short-term fiscal revenue while directly alleviating the government's expenditure burden. However, a reduction in fiscal subsidies would push up fossil fuel prices, causing related economic activities to shrink or even cease, thus triggering a series of chain reactions.

Table 6 summarizes the possible direct and indirect effects of typical dual carbon policies on fiscal revenue and expenditure.

Table 6: Impact Mechanisms of the Dual Carbon Policy on Fiscal Revenue and Expenditure

	Positive Impact	Negative Impact
Fiscal Revenue	• Carbon pricing mechanisms generate new sources of fiscal revenue (direct effect). • The cancellation of tax incentives for fossil fuels will increase tax revenue in the corresponding category (direct effect). • The green transformation of industries creates new growth points for fiscal revenue (indirect effect).	• Decreasing carbon emissions leads to a decrease in carbon pricing revenue (indirect effect). • The decline in traditional fossil fuel consumption has led to a shrinking fuel tax base and a decrease in tax revenue (indirect effect). • The contraction of high-carbon industries leads to a decrease in corporate income tax and value-added tax for related enterprises (indirect effect). • Tax incentives related to green transformation reduce current tax revenue (direct effect).
Fiscal Expenditure	• Investment in green infrastructure (clean energy, smart grids, low-carbon transportation) reduces business operating costs and enhances long-term economic potential (indirect effect). • Reducing subsidies for fossil fuels saves government spending (direct effect).	• Large-scale green investment increases pressure on fiscal spending (direct effect) • Economic restructuring will increase unemployment benefits and social security spending in the short term (indirect effect).

Source: Compiled by the author.

(ii) The Importance of Policy Tool Mix

The analysis from Table 6 shows that **different types of policy tools have different mechanisms and outcomes in affecting fiscal revenue and expenditure. Therefore, specific policy combinations for achieving the dual carbon goals will produce different policy effects.**

Typically, **policy tools that rely heavily on government spending to drive a low-carbon transition often pose greater challenges to fiscal sustainability**. While government investment plays a crucial leading and guarantor role in achieving dual carbon goals, substantial and continuous funding inevitably places higher demands on the government's fundraising capacity and is more likely to increase public debt or exacerbate tax distortions due to forced increases in other taxes (Baur, Bruchez, and Nicol 2021), thus hindering fiscal sustainability. Conversely, **if a carbon pricing mechanism is implemented alongside government investment to provide dedicated funding, the government's fiscal deficit can be effectively mitigated**. A carbon pricing mechanism can strengthen constraints on emissions and expand new sources of revenue. A reasonably priced carbon pricing mechanism can provide relatively stable funding support for government green spending over a certain period. In other words, for the same emissions-reduction effect, increasing the weight of carbon pricing and decreasing the proportion of investment and subsidies in the policy system will be more conducive to maintaining fiscal balance.

In summary, the choice of policy tool mix is crucial to how dual carbon policies affect fiscal sustainability. When designing a low-carbon transition path, governments need to systematically construct a reasonable combination of policy tools to form a complementary dual carbon policy system.

(iii) The Difference Between Short-Term and Medium-to-Long-Term Effects

Another insight from the basic analytical framework is **that the overall impact of the dual carbon policy on fiscal balance will vary across different time horizons**. Considering the mechanisms of various policy tools and the PRC's actual implementation, in the short term, the dual carbon policy will put significant pressure on fiscal expenditures and on insufficient revenue. To ensure the smooth progress of green transformation, large-scale investments in green infrastructure, subsidies for enterprise transformation, and direct support expenditures to households will be concentrated, bringing considerable pressure on fiscal expenditures. However, the tax base of high-energy-consuming industries is gradually shrinking; while emerging green industries are still in the development stage, leading to a continuous decrease in tax revenue in related fields. Simultaneously, the government lacks a carbon pricing mechanism to provide additional financial support. Therefore, the fiscal deficit will continue to widen in the short term.

In the medium- to long-term, with the implementation of the dual carbon policy and the gradual emergence of the effects of green transformation, the structure of fiscal revenue and expenditure will tend to be optimized. On the revenue side, traditional industries will complete low-carbon upgrades, gradually forming new tax revenue growth points, while green industries will continue to develop, becoming an important source of fiscal revenue. At the same time, the structure of fiscal expenditure will gradually adjust, with large-scale investment shifting toward maintenance expenditures and the demand for subsidies from enterprises and households gradually decreasing, thus easing the fiscal burden. In short, technological progress and industrial upgrading driven by the dual carbon policy will sustain economic growth, unleash the potential of fiscal revenue, optimize the expenditure structure, and enhance fiscal sustainability.

Short-Term Fiscal Impact

Given that fiscal and tax policies on dual carbon are mainly based on government expenditures, **this section discusses the scale of financial investment required to achieve dual carbon goals and estimates the corresponding fiscal funding gap, thereby analyzing the impact of achieving dual carbon goals on public finances in the short term**.

(i) Estimating Funding Needs for Achieving the Dual Carbon Goals

Achieving the dual carbon goals represents a comprehensive low-carbon and green transformation of the PRC's economy and society, requiring massive and continuous financial investment. Studies have used both bottom-up and top-down approaches to calculate the financial investment needed for the PRC to achieve the dual carbon goals. The core of the bottom-up approach is to determine the investment required to reduce emissions across sectors of the economy under the scenario of achieving the dual carbon goals, and then sum the financial needs of all sectors to obtain the total funds required. The top-down approach relies on macroeconomic models such as dynamic stochastic general equilibrium (DSGE) or computable general equilibrium (CGE). Based on several assumptions about the economic environment and various economic agents, it uses numerical simulation methods to estimate changes in macroeconomic variables during the process of achieving the dual carbon goals, and then calculates the total funds required for the low-carbon transformation. Table 7 summarizes the estimation results of existing representative studies, specifically:

(a) In its 2021 research report, Carbon Neutrality and Green Finance, the China International Capital Corporation (CICC) calculated the financial investment required for the PRC to achieve carbon neutrality by 2060. The calculation revealed the total financial needs of the seven largest carbon-emitting industries in the PRC during their low-carbon transition, accounting for more than 85% of the country's total carbon emissions. The authors used a bottom-up approach to calculate the financial requirements for each industry to achieve its low-carbon transition goals within the carbon-neutrality framework. Taking the power industry as an example, its green transition requires investment in areas such as power grid infrastructure, energy storage, and clean power generation equipment. Based on the State Grid Corporation of the PRC's proposed carbon neutrality plan, the authors extrapolated investment needs for the power industry to achieve its green transition, accounting for power grid investments and new energy capacity requirements. The summary of investment needs across the seven major industries shows that to achieve carbon neutrality by 2060, **the PRC's total green investment needs from 2021 to 2060 will reach CNY139 trillion. During the period of carbon peaking from 2021 to 2030, the PRC's green investment needs will be approximately CNY2.2 trillion per year, while during the period of carbon neutrality from 2031 to 2060, this figure will be approximately CNY3.9 trillion per year.**

(b) The research team of the Green Finance Professional Committee of the China Finance Society analyzed two scenarios for the PRC's low-carbon transformation in their study: (i) the "existing policy scenario," which summarizes the emissions reduction targets set by various departments and industries based on policies and technology road maps published in 2021; and (ii) the "carbon neutrality scenario," which combines existing policies with the corresponding policies the authors believe are necessary to achieve carbon neutrality. Taking the power sector as an example, the existing policy scenario proposes that coal-fired power units continue to grow slightly during the 14th 5-year plan period, with nonfossil energy accounting for 25% of primary energy consumption by 2030. The carbon neutrality scenario, however, proposes a more aggressive target for decarbonizing the power grid, including a clear timetable for phasing out conventional coal-fired power and accelerating the development of a renewable energy system. After determining the low-carbon transformation targets for key sectors of the economy and society, the study used a bottom-up approach to calculate the total financial investment required to achieve the carbon neutrality scenario over the next 3 decades, starting in 2021. **The results show that from 2021 to 2050, the total green investment required to achieve the dual carbon goals will be CNY487 trillion. This amount includes investment in the low-carbon energy and ecological and environmental protection sectors. If only investment demand in the low-carbon energy sector, comparable to other studies (i.e., the narrow scope investment demand), is considered, the total investment demand will be approximately CNY179 trillion**.[17]

(c) In 2020, the Institute for Climate Change and Sustainable Development at Tsinghua University calculated the green investment needs under different climate policy backgrounds. These included a "policy scenario" based on the PRC's targets under the Paris Agreement; a "reinforced policy scenario" that strengthens indicators such as reducing GDP energy intensity and carbon emissions intensity; and corresponding scenarios based on the 2°C and 1.5°C targets proposed in the Paris Agreement. The study used a bottom-up approach to calculate investment needs in four major sectors: energy supply, industry, buildings, and transport. The total investment required to achieve a low-carbon economic transition was obtained by summing the investment needs of each sector. **The results show that under the policy scenario, the PRC will peak its carbon emissions around 2030, and by 2050, its carbon emissions will be reduced by 10% compared to 2020, requiring a total investment of approximately CNY70 trillion. If the "1.5°C scenario" is taken as the target, the total investment required will be CNY174 trillion**, and by 2050, carbon emissions will be reduced to 20% of 2020 levels.[18]

(d) In 2021, the International Institute of Green Finance at the Central University of Finance and Economics calculated the total capital input required for the PRC to achieve carbon peaking by 2030. In this study, the authors used a top-down approach, constructing an endogenous growth model with biased technological progress, referencing Pan, Chen, and Grubb (2021). Specifically, to characterize the role of policy in low-carbon transformation, the authors introduced financing constraints into the model. Targeted policy support can directly promote the development of the clean sector and encourage research institutions to improve clean production technologies, ultimately achieving a low-carbon economic transformation and realizing carbon peaking and carbon neutrality. Based on the theoretical model, the authors used numerical simulations to obtain the cumulative growth of green factor inputs in the green sector to achieve the global carbon peaking target by 2030, i.e., the investment required to achieve carbon peaking. **The results show that achieving global carbon peaking between 2021 and 2030 will require**

17 The low-carbon sector includes important high-carbon emissions industries such as industry, transport, and construction. Other studies are usually based on these sectors, so the funding needs in the low-carbon sector are highly comparable to other research results.

18 The 1.5°C target is close to the goal of achieving "carbon neutrality" by the mid-21st century.

approximately CNY47.5 trillion in investment. Assuming the PRC's contribution to global economic growth averages 30%, the PRC will need to invest approximately CNY14.2 trillion over this decade.

(e) In 2024, the PRC submitted its First Biennial Transparency Report on Climate Change, which outlines the scale of the country's financial needs for addressing climate change. The funding requirements for achieving carbon neutrality are categorized into those needed for climate change mitigation and adaptation. **Taking both aspects into account, the total funding required for the PRC to reach its carbon peaking goal from 2024 to 2030 is estimated at approximately CNY25.2 trillion, equivalent to an average of CNY3.6 trillion per year. From 2031 to 2060, the total funding need is projected at approximately CNY243 trillion, with an annual average of approximately CNY8.1 trillion.**[19]

Table 7: Estimation Results of Funds Needed to Achieve the Dual Carbon Goals

Source	Method	Scenario	Result
CICC: Carbon Neutrality and Green Finance	Bottom-up approach	Carbon neutrality by 2060	From 2021 to 2060, CNY139 trillion in green investment will be needed, with annual investment of approximately CNY2.2 trillion to CNY3.9 trillion.
The Green Finance Committee of the China Society for Finance and Banking: A Study on the Green Finance Roadmap under the Vision of Carbon Neutrality	Bottom-up approach and top-down approach	Carbon neutrality by 2060	From 2021 to 2050, a total investment of CNY179 trillion–CNY487 trillion will be needed to cover low-carbon energy, ecology, and environmental protection.a
Tsinghua University: Research on the PRC's Long-Term Low-Carbon Development Strategy and Transformation Path	Bottom-up approach	• Policy Scenario • Strengthen policy scenarios • 2°C scenario • 1.5°C scenario	Total investment demand under four different scenarios from 2020 to 2050: • CNY71 trillion • CNY100 trillion • CNY127 trillion • CNY174 trillion
International Institute of Green Finance, Central University of Finance and Economics	Top-down approach	Peak carbon emissions by 2030	CNY14.2 trillion will be needed from 2021 to 2030.
The People's Republic of China First Biennial Transparency Report on Climate Change	Not reported	Peak carbon emissions by 2030 and carbon neutrality by 2060	From 2024 to 2030, CNY25.2 trillion will be needed for climate change mitigation and adaptation; from 2030 to 2060, CNY243 trillion will be needed.

PRC = People's Republic of China, CICC = China International Capital Corporation, CNY = renminbi (yuan).

[a] The report calculated the total green investment required for 2021–2050 based on the PRC's goal of achieving carbon neutrality by 2060.

Source: Compiled by the author.

[19] The report did not disclose its calculation method.

In summary, studies have largely used a narrow scope to calculate the investment required to achieve the dual carbon goals, yielding relatively consistent results: The total investment needed to achieve carbon neutrality is approximately CNY100 trillion–CNY200 trillion.[20] The CICC estimated CNY139 trillion, the Green Finance Committee of the China Finance Society estimates CNY179 trillion, and Tsinghua University estimates CNY174 trillion. The CICC's estimate has been frequently cited by official sources. For example, in 2021, then-Governor of the People's Bank of China, Yi Gang, stated in a speech that "it is estimated that before 2030, the PRC will need to invest CNY2.2 trillion annually in carbon emissions reduction; from 2030 to 2060, it will need to invest CNY3.9 trillion annually."[21] Furthermore, Xie Zhenhua, the PRC's Special Envoy for Climate Change Affairs, pointed out in his speech at the 2022 China International Fair for Trade in Services that the PRC needs more than CNY130 trillion in investment to achieve its dual carbon goals, a conclusion consistent with the CICC's estimate.[22]

If a broad scope is adopted over the narrow scope, incorporating the funding needs of environmental and ecological sectors in achieving carbon neutrality, as well as the additional operating and maintenance costs beyond fixed asset investment resulting from low-carbon transitions in various sectors, the calculated results would be far greater than those obtained under the narrow scope. The PRC's First Biennial Transparency Report on Climate Change indicates that, including funds for climate change adaptation, the total funding requirement would exceed CNY268 trillion from 2024 to 2060. The Green Finance Committee of the China Finance Society estimates that, under the broad scope, the total investment required to achieve carbon neutrality reaches CNY487 trillion. Both results far exceed the investment needs corresponding to the narrow scope.

(ii) Estimated Fiscal Funding Needs for Achieving Dual Carbon Goals

Achieving the dual carbon goals requires an enormous amount of capital, and fiscal funds can only cover a portion of it. As a report by the Green Finance Network—a network of central banks and regulatory bodies—points out, public capital from sources such as fiscal appropriations and official aid cannot be the primary source of funding for climate policy. The report also notes that **experience in developed countries shows that public funds generally account for 10%–30% of climate policy-related funding; for emerging economies and developing countries, public funds should cover 10%–20% of the funding needs to achieve carbon neutrality, to leverage large-scale private capital participation in the green and low-carbon transition**.[23] Regarding the PRC's situation, Jiang and Chen (2023) argue that fiscal funds should cover 10%–15% of the green investment needs to achieve carbon neutrality.

---

20 The narrow scope is mainly reflected in two aspects. First, when considering funding needs, it only covers major carbon-emitting sectors of the economy, such as energy, heavy industry, transport, and construction, without covering environmental protection and ecology, which are equally important in achieving the goal of carbon neutrality. Second, when calculating the funds required for the low-carbon transition process in each sector, it mainly considers the costs required for purchasing or upgrading equipment, without taking into account the subsequent operation and maintenance costs.

21 Central Bank. 2021. Governor Yi Gang of the People's Bank of China attended and addressed a high-level seminar on Green Finance and Climate Policy jointly held by the People's Bank of China and the International Monetary Fund. Micro broadcast. 15 April.

22 *Daily Economic News*. 2022. Xie Zhenhua: The PRC needs more than CNY130 trillion in investment to achieve its "dual carbon" goals; green and low-carbon transformation and innovation will create a huge green market. 2 September.

23 Network for Greening the Financial System. 2023. Scaling Up Blended Finance for Climate Mitigation and Adaptation in Emerging Market and Developing Economies (EMDEs).

Based on this research, this report assumes that fiscal funds should account for 15% of the total investment required for carbon neutrality. Based on this proportion and combined with the total investment funding requirements, **the PRC's annual fiscal investment required to achieve carbon neutrality is approximately CNY521.3 billion to CNY2.435 trillion.**[24] Among the fiscal expenditure data disclosed by the Government of the PRC, energy conservation and environmental protection expenditures are the most directly related to the carbon neutrality target. This data includes fiscal expenditures in multiple areas such as supporting renewable energy development, environmental protection and pollution control, and ecological restoration.

Therefore, **its calculation method is closer to the broad scope standard used in the previous calculation of the carbon neutrality target funding requirements**. To ensure relative comparability of the data, the following analysis compares the average annual fiscal funding requirement under the broad scope standard (i.e., CNY2.44 trillion) with the actual carbon neutrality fiscal expenditure (i.e., energy conservation and environmental protection expenditure). Figure 5 shows that **from 2020 to 2024, the average annual national fiscal expenditure on carbon-related initiatives was approximately CNY570 billion. Compared to the average annual fiscal funding requirement of CNY2.435 trillion, there is a funding gap of approximately CNY1.87 trillion (accounting for 1.38% of the 2024 GDP)**. If the proportion of fiscal funding required relative to total funding for carbon-related targets exceeds 15%, the funding gap will widen further. Furthermore, Figure 5 indicates that since 2020, the actual intensity of carbon-related fiscal expenditure has shown a downward trend; therefore, this funding gap is likely to widen.

Figure 5: Total Expenditure on Energy Conservation and Environmental Protection in the People's Republic of China

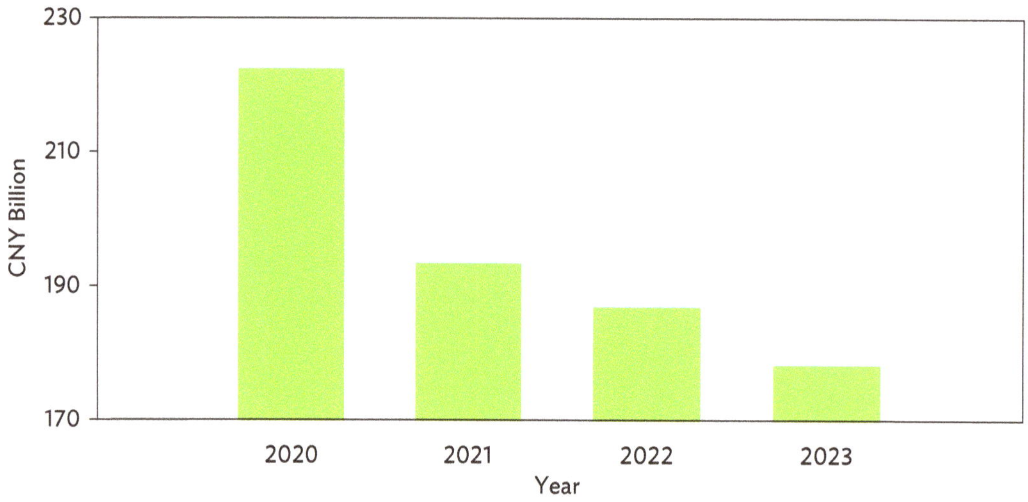

CNY = yuan.

Source: Census and Economic Information Center Database (accessed January 2026).

[24] Based on CICC's calculation of a total funding requirement of CNY139 trillion under the narrow definition, the PRC would need approximately CNY521.3 billion in fiscal investment annually to achieve dual carbon emissions. Based on the calculation of a total funding requirement of CNY487 trillion under the broad definition by the Green Finance Professional Committee of the China Finance Society, the PRC would need approximately CNY2.44 trillion in fiscal investment annually to achieve dual carbon emissions.

(iii) Fiscal Funding Gaps for Dual Carbon Goals in Various Regions

The dual carbon goals ultimately need to be achieved through regional efforts. Therefore, regions with higher carbon emissions will inevitably bear a heavier emissions reduction burden and invest more fiscal funds. Based on this, **this paper uses each province's carbon emissions as a proportion of the national total to allocate the national dual carbon fiscal funding needs proportionally to the provincial level and considers this as an approximation of the fiscal funds each province needs to invest to achieve its dual carbon goals**. Table 8 reports the calculation results and the actual scale of dual carbon fiscal expenditure (i.e., energy conservation and environmental protection expenditure) in each province.[25] The results show that all regions except Beijing have a dual carbon fiscal expenditure gap. **The region with the largest gap is Ningxia, where the dual carbon fiscal expenditure gap accounts for 8% of local GDP. Besides Ningxia, Inner Mongolia, and Xinjiang, other provinces also face significant dual carbon fiscal expenditure gaps. The main reason is that these provinces are major fossil energy-producing areas in the PRC**, with a strong dependence on high-carbon-emitting industries, and are high-carbon-emitting regions, leading to greater emissions reduction expenditure needs. Gansu, Guangxi, Guizhou, and Heilongjiang—four regions with relatively small total carbon emissions—also face significant expenditure gaps, primarily due to their low fiscal spending intensity on carbon and emissions reduction. In contrast, Beijing, Chongqing, Qinghai, and Shanghai—four provinces and/or municipalities—have the smallest expenditure gaps, mainly because their industrial structures include a lower proportion of high-carbon-emitting industries, thereby reducing their need for emissions-reduction spending.

Table 8: Estimated Fiscal Funding Gaps for Dual Carbon Goals in Different Provinces

Province	Carbon Emissions Percentage (%)	Energy Conservation and Environmental Protection Expenditure Needs (CNY100 million)	Energy Conservation and Environmental Protection Expenditures (CNY100 million)	Fiscal Gaps to Local GDP (%)
Ningxia	2.17	502	76	8.00
Inner Mongolia	7.70	1,782	178	6.51
Xinjiang	4.60	1,063	133	4.87
Shanxi	5.52	1,276	242	4.03
Hebei	7.56	1,748	321	3.25
Liaoning	4.61	1,066	87	3.24
Heilongjiang	2.40	554	154	2.52
Gansu	1.72	397	146	2.11
Guizhou	2.21	511	129	1.83
Guangxi	2.45	566	70	1.82
Shandong	8.07	1,867	209	1.80

continued on next page

[25] Based on actual data, the PRC's energy conservation and environmental protection expenditures mainly rely on local government revenue, with central government spending accounting for less than 5% of this expenditure. Therefore, when calculating the dual carbon fiscal funding needs of each province, we adjusted the total local dual carbon fiscal funding needs to CNY2.435 billion × (1–5%) = CNY2.313 billion. Due to the lack of relevant carbon emissions data, the Tibet Autonomous Region is not included in the calculation.

Table 8 *continued*

Province	Carbon Emissions Percentage (%)	Energy Conservation and Environmental Protection Expenditure Needs (CNY100 million)	Energy Conservation and Environmental Protection Expenditures (CNY100 million)	Fiscal Gaps to Local GDP (%)
Jilin	1.64	379	152	1.67
Tianjin	1.34	310	34	1.65
Henan	4.64	1,073	179	1.51
Anhui	3.87	894	194	1.49
Shaanxi	3.20	741	245	1.47
Jiangsu	7.20	1,665	247	1.11
Hubei	3.27	756	188	1.02
Yunnan	1.93	446	154	0.97
Zhejiang	4.04	935	188	0.90
Hunan	2.69	623	170	0.90
Fujian	2.62	607	120	0.89
Jiangxi	1.96	453	249	0.63
Sichuan	2.70	624	254	0.62
Hainan	0.39	91	45	0.61
Guangdong	5.43	1,256	445	0.60
Chongqing	1.42	329	185	0.48
Shanghai	1.57	362	255	0.23
Qinghai	0.49	112	109	0.08
Beijing	0.63	145	221	(0.17)

( ) = negative, CNY = renminbi (yuan), GDP = gross domestic product.

Note: The gap is calculated as follows: Gap = (expenditure demand – actual expenditure) / GDP.

Source: Author's calculation.

Medium- and Long-Term Fiscal Impacts

Research on the impact of climate policies on fiscal sustainability mostly employs general equilibrium models or reduced-form estimation models. This section discusses the medium- and long-term impacts of the PRC's dual carbon policy on fiscal sustainability, based on conclusions drawn from literature using dynamic or computable general equilibrium models to estimate the impacts of global or national climate policies. Simultaneously, using quantitative indicators for carbon peaking set by various provinces, a reduced-form model is used to estimate the impact of the dual carbon policy on fiscal revenue and expenditure.

(i) General Equilibrium Analysis

Table 9 summarizes the main scenarios and conclusions of existing studies using general equilibrium models to study the impact of carbon neutrality policies on fiscal sustainability. Although the specific model methods and the simulation scenarios differ, these studies have yielded similar core conclusions that are equally applicable to the Chinese scenario: (a) Adopting a carbon neutrality policy dominated by fiscal expenditure will lead to a significant increase in the government debt ratio and a crowding-out effect on consumption, making it difficult to achieve fiscal sustainability; (b) Adopting a reasonable combination of revenue and expenditure policies, including carbon taxes, can promote the achievement of carbon neutrality while maintaining fiscal sustainability; and (c) Achieving the goal of carbon neutrality and maintaining fiscal sustainability inevitably requires the support of additional revenue-generating fiscal instruments. Specifically:

(a) Black et al. (2024) used the climate policy assessment tool model to calculate the impact of achieving carbon neutrality goals in multiple countries and regions worldwide on fiscal sustainability. Based on the goal of limiting global warming to no more than 2°C as proposed in the Paris Climate Agreement, if policies are mainly based on fiscal spending, infrastructure investment, and compensation to residents, they will lead to increased fiscal deficits across various countries. Simulation results show that by 2030, expenditure-based climate policies will widen the fiscal deficits of France and the UK by approximately 1.0% of GDP; Germany's fiscal situation is even more severe, with the deficit widening by approximately 1.5% of GDP. If a carbon price cap is set, the fiscal sustainability of these countries will further deteriorate; for example, Germany's fiscal deficit will widen by approximately 2.0% of GDP.

    The study also calculated the fiscal impact on the PRC's efforts to achieve carbon neutrality. Simulation results show that infrastructure investment needs, fiscal expenditures to compensate households, and fiscal pressure from reduced fuel tax revenue during the carbon neutrality process will **result in a fiscal deficit of approximately 1.5% of GDP in the PRC by 2030. This means that relying solely on fiscal expenditure policies to achieve carbon neutrality cannot maintain the PRC's fiscal sustainability**. The simulation also indicates that if the PRC fully implements carbon pricing, its high carbon emissions can generate substantial fiscal revenue; assuming a carbon price of CNY80 in the PRC by 2030, this will generate approximately 2.5% of GDP, covering the fiscal deficit during the carbon neutrality process. Even with a capped carbon price, the PRC can still generate approximately 1.5% of GDP in fiscal revenue by 2030 using carbon pricing.[26] These simulation results demonstrate that, under a reasonable policy mix, the PRC can maintain fiscal sustainability while pursuing carbon neutrality.

(b) Fouré et al. (2023) used a global computable general equilibrium (CGE) model to analyze the changes in net fiscal revenue in 2030 and 2050 under the scenario of achieving carbon neutrality by mid-century. The simulation results show that **under the existing policy mix, which is dominated by fiscal expenditure, carbon neutrality will exert significant fiscal pressure on all countries and regions worldwide, worsening fiscal sustainability**. By 2030, most countries and regions will experience a decline in net fiscal revenue, primarily due to the large fiscal expenditure required to fund household subsidies. Household subsidies account for approximately 0.8% of global GDP. Although carbon taxes can generate additional fiscal revenue, they are still insufficient to cover

26 It is important to emphasize that this article only considers the situation up to 2030, that is, before carbon peaking. During the transition from carbon peaking to carbon neutrality, reductions in carbon tax revenue will have a heterogeneous impact on fiscal sustainability.

the additional expenditure demand driven by climate policies dominated by fiscal expenditure, ultimately leading to a decrease in global net income of approximately 0.4% of GDP. When carbon neutrality is achieved in 2050, government net revenue will further decline, and the fiscal sustainability problem will become more severe. This is mainly because revenue from carbon pricing tools gradually decreases as carbon emissions decline, while subsidies to households affected by the transition continue to increase, ultimately leading to a sustained increase in fiscal pressure. By 2050, global net fiscal revenue will decline by 1.8% of GDP, affecting all countries and regions worldwide. North America will be most affected, with a significant drop in carbon tax revenue and a substantial increase in the need for household subsidies, resulting in a decrease in net fiscal revenue of approximately 3% of GDP. Some Asian countries, including the PRC, will maintain some carbon tax revenue, thus experiencing a smaller decline in net fiscal revenue, approximately 0.5% of GDP. These results suggest that climate policies primarily relying on subsidies and direct investment are not conducive to maintaining fiscal sustainability in achieving carbon neutrality. Even if carbon pricing tools generate substantial additional fiscal revenue, they will still be insufficient to cover the additional expenditure demands arising from these policies.

Another simulation result from the study indicates that **if governments choose to strengthen carbon pricing while weakening spending policies such as subsidies and investment, this policy combination can alleviate fiscal pressure while achieving the goal of carbon neutrality**. By 2050, global net fiscal revenue would decrease by only about 0.5% of GDP, far lower than the baseline simulation result for a policy primarily based on fiscal spending. Compared to policies primarily based on fiscal spending, this policy combination maintains better policy fiscal sustainability while achieving the goal of carbon neutrality.

(c) The International Monetary Fund (IMF) (2023) constructed a dynamic general equilibrium model comprising representative advanced and emerging economies to simulate changes in government debt as the 2050 carbon neutrality target is achieved. The results show that, with a policy primarily based on fiscal spending, government debt in advanced economies would increase by approximately 45% of GDP relative to the scenario without such a policy, while emerging economies would face an increase of approximately 50% of GDP. This indicates that a fiscal spending-based approach to carbon neutrality would lead to excessively high levels of government debt, worsening fiscal sustainability. The study also simulated a scenario with a capped carbon price policy and a low-intensity fiscal spending policy. Under this policy combination, the cumulative increase in government debt by 2050 would be approximately 12% in advanced and 25% in emerging economies, representing a lower fiscal burden compared to a fiscal spending-based policy. While these policies have a relatively small impact on fiscal sustainability, they also lead to insufficient policy strength. Simulation results show that under a limited carbon price setting ($75 for developed economies and $45 for emerging economies), this policy combination can only reduce carbon emissions by 40% by 2050 relative to current levels. To achieve carbon neutrality, the carbon price must be raised to $280, a level that most countries cannot afford. Therefore, advancing the carbon neutrality goal while maintaining fiscal sustainability inevitably requires support from other revenue-generating fiscal instruments.

(d) Seghini and Dees (2024) used a dynamic general model involving the corporate, government, and household sectors to simulate the impact of the 2060 carbon neutrality target on Italy's fiscal sustainability. The authors incorporated fiscal tools such as direct investment, bonds, carbon taxes, and subsidies into the model and analyzed the different policy impacts of various policy combinations. The model also considered government debt risk: when the government debt ratio is high, the risk of debt default increases, and to maintain fiscal balance, the government needs to adjust tax rates promptly to prevent continuous deterioration of fiscal sustainability. The authors considered changes in fiscal sustainability under three different policy scenarios in the model:

- **Using only the carbon tax tool**. To achieve carbon neutrality by 2060, the carbon price must be raised to CNY800 by 2030 and maintained at CNY1,000 from 2045 onward. While a high level of carbon tax increases fiscal revenue and reduces government debt levels and debt risks, the significantly increased production costs also lead to a decline in total economic output. By 2060, GDP will decline by about 1% and consumption by about 3.5%, indicating that **relying solely on the carbon tax to achieve carbon neutrality will entail enormous policy costs**.
- **Using only direct fiscal investment as a policy tool**. In this scenario, although direct fiscal investment can boost GDP growth, it also **leads to rapid short-term accumulation of government debt, increasing the government debt ratio by 7% and the risk of debt default by 10%, which seriously deteriorates fiscal sustainability**. At the same time, large-scale direct investment also leads to a "crowding-out effect" on consumption, which will decline by about 1.7% in the short term. Furthermore, in the middle and later stages of the transition process, to maintain fiscal balance, the government will raise tax rates to expand revenue, which also brings additional policy costs.
- **Adopting a policy combining a carbon tax and fiscal subsidies**. From the perspective of the entire process of achieving carbon neutrality, this policy can better maintain the relative stability of government debt, with the government debt ratio increasing by only 3% in the short term. Although fiscal subsidies have a weaker effect on GDP growth than direct investment policies, their short-term impact on consumption is also relatively weak. In summary, this type of policy combination can help achieve carbon neutrality while maintaining fiscal sustainability.

(5) Since 2021, the UK's Office for Budget Responsibility (OBR) has been analyzing the impact of climate change risks on the UK's fiscal sustainability in its Fiscal Risks and Sustainability Report, employing a bottom-up approach to calculate the fiscal costs of climate policies and their impact on government debt.[27] OBR's 2024 calculations show that to achieve the 2050 net-zero carbon emissions target—if the government fully implements a carbon tax—the cumulative increase in government debt from 2020 to 2050 would reach 20% of GDP. If a comprehensive carbon tax policy is not

[27] This method sets different targets for different fields and industries, such as the electrification rate and the proportion of clean energy in the transport sector, calculates the investment amount required to achieve the transformation target in each field, and sums them up to obtain the total transformation cost.

implemented, the government will incur additional policy costs.[28] The report also considers other possible policy combinations. If the government can quickly implement a carbon tax policy and introduce a vehicle driving tax to offset lost fuel tax revenue, the cumulative increase in government debt by 2050 will be negative. This means that the entire economic transition phase will not impose additional debt burdens on government finances; instead, it could reduce government debt by 10% of GDP, improving fiscal sustainability. Finally, the simulation results show that **the timing of policy implementation is also extremely critical**: If the government delays the implementation of fiscal policies, the cumulative new debt required to achieve carbon neutrality by 2050 will reach 40% of GDP, far above the baseline.

Table 9: Research on the Impacts of Climate Policy on Fiscal Sustainability

Source	Method	Scenario	Main Findings
Black et al. (2024)	The CPAT model was jointly developed by the IMF and the World Bank	Based on the goal of limiting global warming to no more than 2°C, simulations of the 2030 scenario are performed. The research scope includes countries and regions such as the PRC, the United States, the European Union, and the African Union.	• Without other tax tools, the debt ratios of developed countries would increase by 1%–2%. • If a reasonable international transfer payment system is established, developing countries can reduce their fiscal deficits and enhance their fiscal sustainability.
Fouré et al. (2023)	CGE model	Scenario for achieving carbon neutrality by 2050. The research covers a global scope, primarily focusing on OECD countries.	• If only existing policy tools are used, net fiscal revenue will decrease by 1.8%. • If carbon pricing can be increased and spending policies can be weakened, fiscal pressure can be reduced.
IMF (2023)	DSGE model	Scenario for achieving carbon neutrality by 2050. Representative models, studies based on global circumstances.	• If a spending-driven policy is maintained, government debt will increase by 45%–50% of GDP. • If a globally collaborative carbon pricing model is introduced, along with other fiscal revenue tools and transfer payment systems, debt growth can be reduced to 10%–15% of GDP.

continued on next page

[28] The UK's carbon pricing tool is mainly the Emissions Trading System (ETS), which only covers energy-intensive industries, including the power generation sector. Furthermore, the government still issues a large number of free allowances, meaning that the UK has not actually established a comprehensive carbon tax system.

Table 9 *continued*

Source	Method	Scenario	Main Findings
Seghini and Dees (2024)	DSGE model	Scenario for achieving carbon neutrality by 2050. The research scope only includes Italy.	• By adopting an investment-led policy, government debt increased by 7% in the short term, and debt risk increased by 10%. • Using carbon tax tools alone can significantly improve fiscal sustainability in the short term, but will severely suppress private sector consumption. • Adopting a policy that combines carbon taxes and targeted subsidies can maintain stable levels of government debt with minimal loss of welfare to the private sector.
OBR[a]	Bottom-up approach[b]	Scenario for achieving carbon neutrality by 2050. The research scope is limited to the United Kingdom.	• Using only existing policy tools, the government debt ratio (debt/GDP) will increase by 20% by 2050. • If a comprehensive carbon tax could be implemented earlier, along with policy tools including a driving tax, it would be possible to reduce the government debt ratio by 10% and ensure fiscal sustainability.

PRC = People's Republic of China, CGE = computable general equilibrium, CPAT = climate policy assessment tool, DSGE = dynamic stochastic general equilibrium, GDP = gross domestic product, IMF = International Monetary Fund, OBR = The UK Office for Budget Responsibility, OECD = Organisation for Economic Co-operation and Development.

Notes:

[a] Government of the United Kingdom, Office for Budget Responsibility. 2024. *Fiscal Risk Report*. September.

[b] This method sets different targets for different fields and industries, such as the electrification rate and the proportion of clean energy in the transport sector, calculates the investment amount required to achieve the transformation target in each field, and sums them up to obtain the total transformation cost.

Source: Compiled by the author.

(ii) Reduced-Form Model Estimation

Based on the quantitative emissions reduction targets (specifically, the share of nonfossil energy and energy consumption per unit of GDP) established in the dual carbon goal implementation plans at the national and provincial levels, as systematically sorted out in this report, this section combines historical fiscal revenue and expenditure data and employs a multivariate time series ARIMAX model to forecast the fiscal sustainability conditions when the PRC and selected representative provinces achieve the carbon peak by 2030. It should be noted that the national and provincial governments have set only the target value for carbon peaking in 2030 and have not yet determined the target value for carbon neutrality.

Specifically, the ARIMAX model is a time series forecasting tool. Its core idea is to improve forecast accuracy by introducing external explanatory variables (X) based on the historical patterns of time series data. Based on this, this paper uses fiscal revenue (Gov_rev) and fiscal expenditure (Gov_exp) as the predicted variables, and per capita GDP (GDP/Population), the proportion of coal energy consumption in total energy consumption (Coal_ratio), and energy consumption per unit of GDP (Energy GDP) as external explanatory variables to predict the changes in fiscal revenue and expenditure for the whole country and representative provinces by 2030. Per capita GDP represents the intrinsic impact of regional economic development on changes in fiscal revenue and expenditure, while the proportion of coal energy consumption in total primary energy consumption and energy consumption per unit of GDP capture the impact of changes in carbon emissions and energy efficiency on fiscal revenue and expenditure.

In the specific forecasting process, this study followed two steps: (a) based on historical sample data (i.e., 2000–2022), the ARIMAX model was used to estimate the impact coefficients of each external explanatory variable on the changes in fiscal revenue and expenditure; (b) based on the values of each external explanatory variable after 2022 and the parameters obtained in step (a), the study forecast the changes in fiscal revenue and expenditure from 2023 to 2030.

Three points need to be explained regarding the data: (a) The future value of GDP is calculated based on the World Bank's forecast of the PRC's GDP growth rate from 2024 to 2060, and it is assumed that the GDP growth rate of each province is synchronized with the national growth rate; the future value of the total population is calculated based on the UN's forecast of the PRC's future population growth rate, and it is assumed that the population growth rate of each province is synchronized with the national growth rate;[29] (b) The future value of coal energy consumption ratio is calculated by adjusting the nonfossil energy ratio target value determined by the implementation plan of the dual carbon goals of each province (Figure 2) and the average value of coal energy consumption in the total fossil energy consumption of each province from 2020 to 2023; and (c) Since the implementation plan of the dual carbon goals of each province does not directly disclose the energy consumption target value per unit of GDP when the carbon peak is reached in 2030, the study used the energy consumption target value per unit of GDP set at the national level when the carbon peak is reached in 2030 as the basis, and adjust the calculation by combining the relative coefficient of the average energy consumption per unit of GDP of each province and the national average from 2020 to 2023.

Based on this method, Figures 6–11 present the estimation results for the whole country (Figure 6) and representative provinces for coal energy intensity regions (Inner Mongolia, Figure 7), the Northeast Region of the PRC (Liaoning, Figure 8), the Southwest Region of the PRC (Sichuan, Figure 9), the Northwest Region of the PRC (Gansu, Figure 10), and the Southeast Region of the PRC (Guangdong, Figure 11). In the corresponding graphs of the estimation results, **solid lines represent actual fiscal revenue and expenditure figures, and dashed lines represent predicted figures**. To verify the effectiveness of the ARIMAX model's predictions, the study also reports the actual and predicted values of fiscal revenue and expenditure for 2020–2022 (i.e., after the implementation of the dual carbon goals) for comparison. Specifically:

(a) **Nationwide situation**. By comparing the actual and projected values of fiscal revenue and expenditure from 2020 to 2022, the ARIMAX model's predictions closely match the actual values, verifying its effectiveness. As shown in Figure 6, after 2022, national fiscal expenditure (blue dashed line) continued to grow, while national fiscal revenue (red dashed line) showed a slow downward trend, further widening the national fiscal revenue and expenditure gap. **It is projected that by 2030, the ratio of the gap between national fiscal expenditure and fiscal revenue to GDP will rise from 5% in 2022 to 11%.**

[29] The World Bank's GDP growth forecasts for the PRC from 2024 to 2060 are shown in Appendix, Table A3. The UN's forecasts for the PRC's future population growth rate are shown in Appendix, Table A4

Figure 6: Nationwide Forecast of Fiscal Revenue and Expenditure by 2030

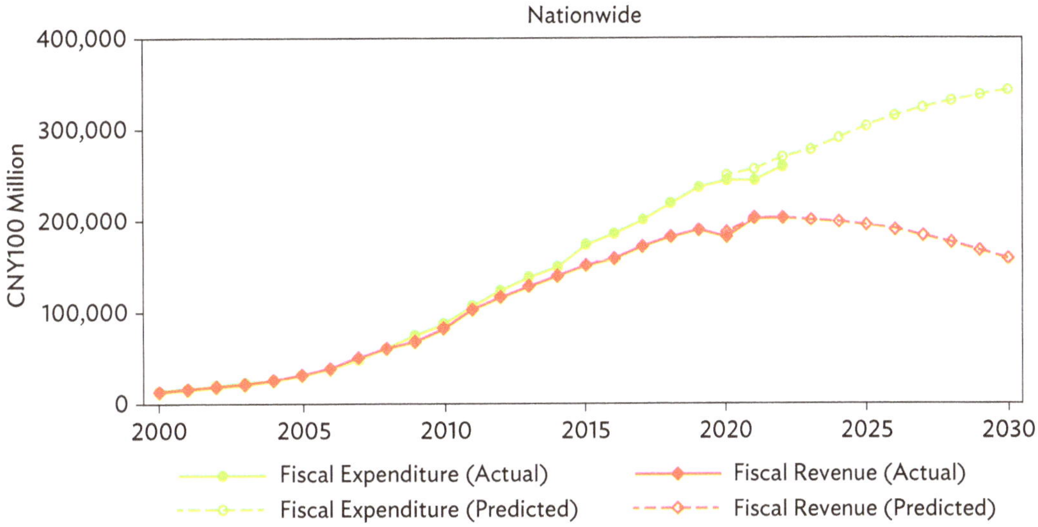

CNY = yuan.
Source: Author's calculation.

(b) **Major coal energy province: Inner Mongolia**. Inner Mongolia is a crucial energy and strategic resource base in the PRC. Its industrial and energy consumption structures have long been dominated by coal; its proven coal reserves account for more than one-quarter of the national total, and it has developed downstream industries such as coal-fired power and coal chemicals based on these resources. Due to its resource advantages, coal consumption in Inner Mongolia has consistently accounted for more than 80% of its total energy consumption, and its energy consumption per unit of GDP is also higher than the national average. At the same time, the energy industry in Inner Mongolia makes a significant contribution to tax revenue, especially in resource-based cities like Ordos, where the government's finances are highly dependent on coal. This high proportion of coal consumption and the government's heavy reliance on coal pose serious challenges to Inner Mongolia in achieving its dual carbon goals and promoting industrial transformation and development.

In 2022, the Inner Mongolia government officially issued the Inner Mongolia Autonomous Region Carbon Peak Implementation Plan, which states that by 2025, the proportion of nonfossil energy consumption will be increased to 18%, and the proportion of coal consumption will be reduced to below 75%; by 2030, the proportion of nonfossil energy consumption will be further increased to about 25%, ensuring that carbon peaking is achieved before 2030. To achieve this goal, Inner Mongolia needs to strictly control the growth of coal consumption and also invest heavily in developing new energy sources such as wind power and photovoltaics. According to the ARIMAX model, the fiscal revenue and expenditure gap in Inner Mongolia is expected to widen further (Figure 7). By 2030, the ratio of the gap between fiscal expenditure and fiscal revenue to GDP in Inner Mongolia will increase from 15.2% in 2023 to 27.5%.

Figure 7: Inner Mongolia: Forecast of Fiscal Revenue and Expenditure by 2030

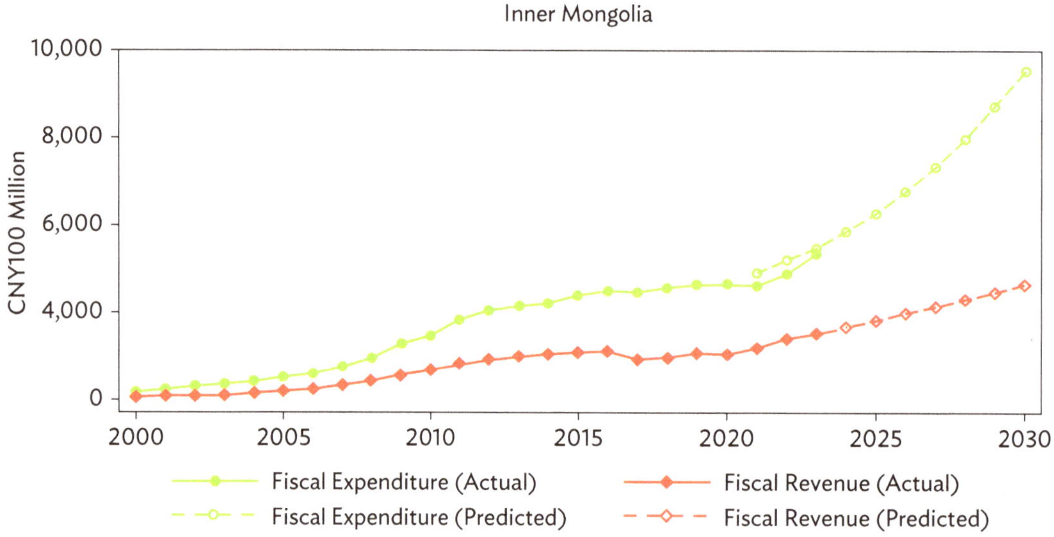

CNY = yuan.
Source: Author's calculation.

(c) **Northeast Region: Taking Liaoning as an example**. As a former heavy industrial base in the Northeast Region of the PRC, Liaoning boasts a massive steel, petrochemical, and equipment manufacturing industry. Furthermore, Liaoning experiences severe winters, resulting in a huge demand for heating. All of these factors contribute to Liaoning's enormous energy needs. However, Liaoning's energy mainly comes from other provinces or countries, exhibiting a high degree of external dependence. Its dependence on foreign sources for coal, oil, and natural gas is close to or exceeds 80%. This high energy dependence makes it more difficult for Liaoning to control its own carbon emissions.

To achieve its carbon peaking target by 2030, Liaoning Province's carbon peaking implementation plan sets clear objectives: by 2025, the proportion of nonfossil energy consumption will reach approximately 13.7%; energy consumption per unit of GDP will decrease by 14.5% compared to 2020; by 2030, the proportion of nonfossil energy consumption will increase to approximately 20%, achieving the carbon peaking target. Given Liaoning Province's high dependence on foreign energy, its carbon peaking efforts are severely constrained by its own economic structure, technological level, and public needs: Liaoning Province must first construct large-scale clean energy systems such as wind power, photovoltaics, nuclear power, and energy storage to ensure that these new energy systems can stably replace coal-fired power before gradually reducing coal imports. Furthermore, Liaoning Province needs to invest heavily in low-carbon technological transformation of traditional heavy industries while cultivating new green industries, a long and costly process. During this process, the growth rate of fiscal expenditure will exceed that of fiscal revenue, thereby affecting fiscal sustainability. According to the ARIMAX model, Liaoning Province's fiscal expenditure growth rate will exceed its fiscal revenue growth rate, further widening the fiscal revenue–expenditure gap (Figure 8). **By 2030, the ratio of fiscal expenditure to fiscal revenue to GDP in Liaoning Province will increase from 12.6% in 2023 to 33%**.

Figure 8: Liaoning: Forecast of Fiscal Revenue and Expenditure by 2030

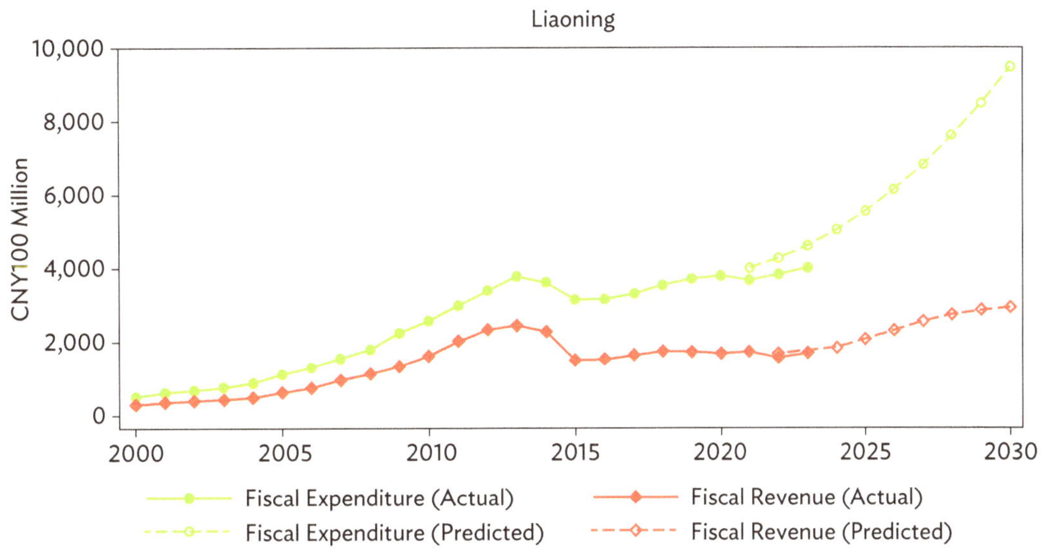

CNY = yuan.

Source: Author's calculation.

(d) **Southwest Region.** Taking Sichuan as an example. As a major economic province and a clean energy base in the western region of the PRC, Sichuan's carbon peaking efforts are of great significance to the nation's goal of achieving dual carbon emissions. Although Sichuan still has a number of energy-intensive industries such as steel, cement, and chemicals, it has unique advantages in achieving its dual carbon goals. First, Sichuan is rich in clean energy resources and is the largest hydropower base in the country; second, Sichuan has successfully cultivated green, low-carbon advantageous industries such as crystalline silicon photovoltaics and power batteries. Therefore, the difficulty for Sichuan in reducing carbon emissions is not a lack of clean energy, but rather how to break the path of dependence on its industrial structure and ensure a stable supply of clean energy, which also requires substantial financial investment.

According to the Sichuan Province Carbon Peak Implementation Plan, Sichuan plans to achieve a nonfossil energy consumption share of approximately 41.5% by 2025, and reduce energy consumption per unit of GDP by more than 14% compared to 2020. By 2030, the nonfossil energy consumption share will increase to approximately 43.5%, successfully achieving the carbon peak target before 2030. According to the ARIMAX model, **in 2030, the gap between Sichuan's fiscal expenditure and fiscal revenue is projected to remain stable at about 12% of GDP, consistent with the level observed in 2023** (Figure 9).

Figure 9: Sichuan: Forecast of Fiscal Revenue and Expenditure by 2030

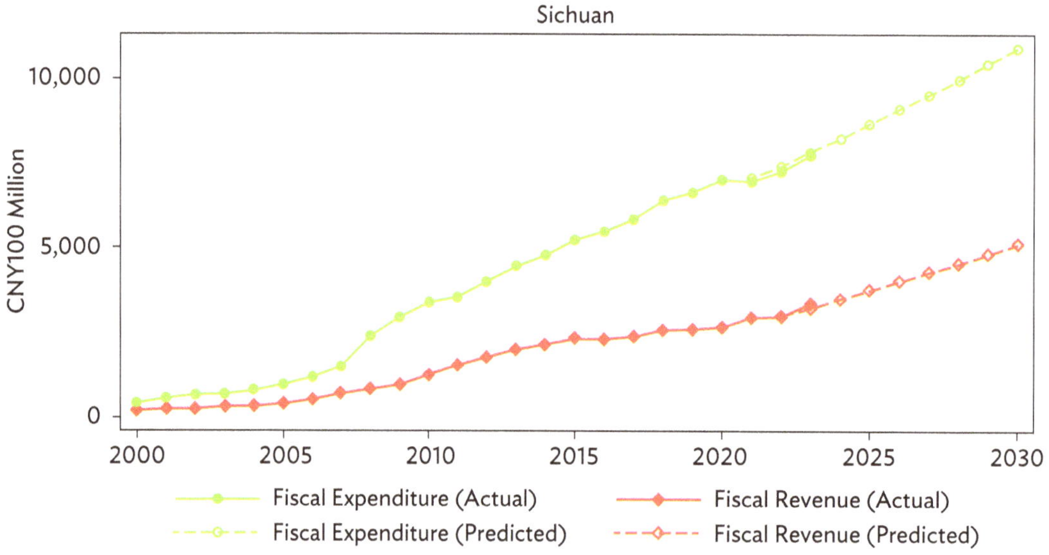

CNY = yuan.

Source: Author's calculation.

(e) **Northwest Region: Taking Gansu as an example.** Gansu Province has traditionally high-energy-consuming industries such as petrochemicals, nonferrous metals, and iron and steel metallurgy, resulting in relatively high energy consumption per unit of GDP. Although Gansu has advantages in new energy sources such as wind and solar power, its coal-dominated energy structure is unlikely to change fundamentally in the short term. These high-energy-consuming industries face multiple constraints in technology, funding, and market access during the green and low-carbon transformation process. Gansu's technology level in low-carbon emissions is still relatively underdeveloped, and its overall modern industrial system is not fully developed, requiring significant investment in the cultivation and development of low-carbon industries. At the same time, Gansu's urbanization rate is low; in 2020, the urbanization rate of the province's permanent residents was 52.23%, 11.66 percentage points lower than the national average, indicating that urbanization-driven development will put enormous pressure on the implementation of the dual carbon strategy for carbon reduction and emissions reduction. Finally, as an economically underdeveloped region, Gansu faces shortcomings such as an aging and low-level industrial base, a lack of distinctive industries, a lack of leading enterprises, and limited development of small and medium-sized private enterprises, resulting in weak fiscal revenue growth and a significant funding gap for its green and low-carbon transformation.

According to the Gansu Province Carbon Peak Implementation Plan, by 2025, the proportion of nonfossil energy consumption will reach 30%, and energy consumption per unit of GDP will decrease by 12.5% compared to 2020; by 2030, the proportion of nonfossil energy consumption will reach approximately 35%, striving to achieve the carbon peak target. According to the ARIMAX model, the fiscal revenue and expenditure gap in Gansu Province is projected to widen further (Figure 10). **By 2030, the gap between Sichuan's fiscal expenditure and fiscal revenue as a percentage of GDP will increase from 29.7% in 2023 to 33%.**

Figure 10: Gansu: Forecast of Fiscal Revenue and Expenditure by 2030

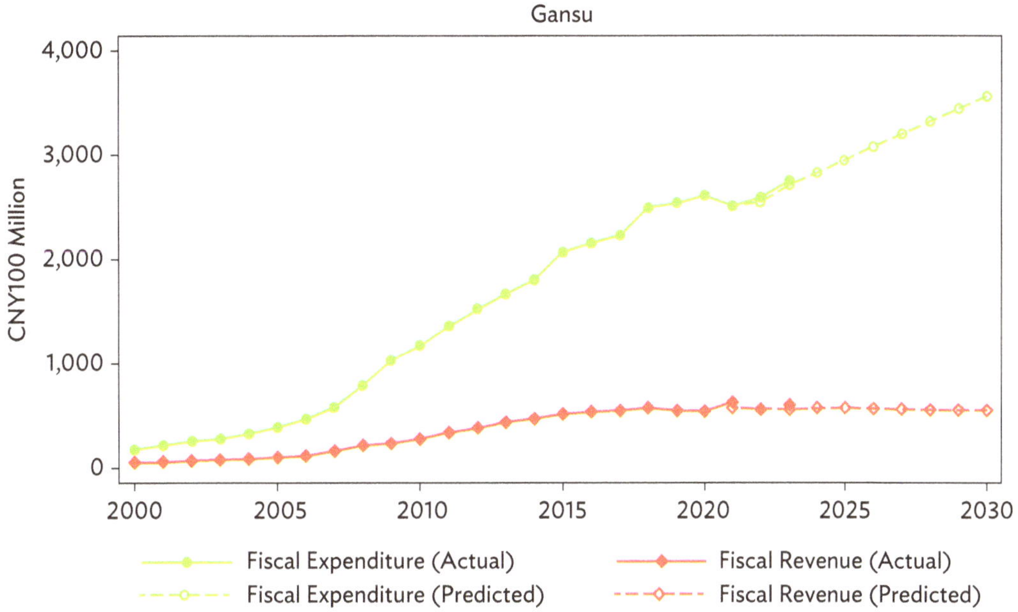

CNY = yuan.

Source: Author's calculation.

(f) **Southeast Region: Taking Guangdong as an example.** As a major economic province, Guangdong faces opportunities to coordinate its economic development pattern and its carbon peaking target, as well as numerous challenges that require balancing. First, Guangdong has a large economy, and fossil fuels still account for a relatively high proportion of its total energy consumption. This means that the contradiction between the overall pressure to reduce energy consumption and emissions will remain prominent. Although Guangdong has been actively exploring and improving its carbon market since 2013, problems such as insufficient liquidity and price volatility still exist. In addition, in August 2025, Guangdong Province for the first time explicitly defined carbon allowances as legal collateral at the provincial level and pioneered a dual registration model under the People's Bank of China Unified Registration and Publicity System for Movable Property Financing and the Provincial Trading Platform. Despite these innovations, the business scale of carbon finance remains relatively small.

According to the Guangdong Province Carbon Peak Implementation Plan, by 2025, the proportion of nonfossil energy consumption will reach more than 32%; by 2030, the proportion will reach approximately 35%, and the control levels of energy consumption per unit of GDP and carbon dioxide emissions per unit of GDP will continue to be among the highest in the country, successfully achieving the carbon peak target. According to the ARIMAX model, the fiscal revenue and expenditure gap in Guangdong Province is projected to continue to widen (Figure 11). **By 2030, the gap between Guangdong's fiscal expenditure and fiscal revenue as a percentage of GDP will rise from 3.4% in 2023 to 5.4%.**

Figure 11: Guangdong: Forecast of Fiscal Revenue and Expenditure by 2030

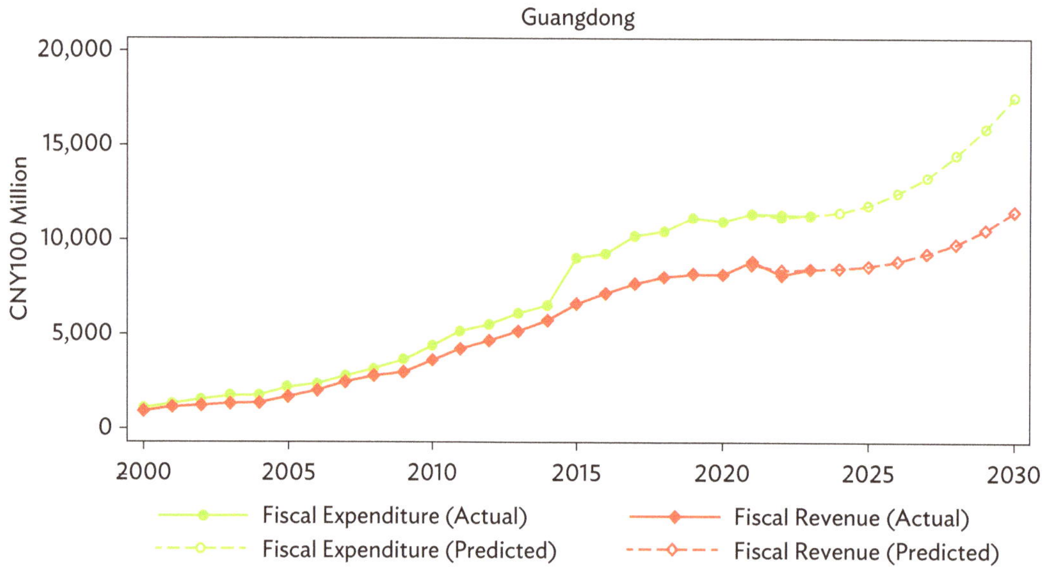

CNY = yuan.

Source: Author's calculation.

In summary, the model estimations indicate that **to achieve the 2030 carbon peak target, the fiscal revenue gap in the PRC and most provinces will increase to varying degrees (ranging from 2% to 20%). For most provinces, this poses a serious challenge to future fiscal sustainability**. It should be noted that the quantitative results from the general equilibrium and reduced-form models in this analysis rely on the validity of the relevant model assumptions; therefore, interpretation of the specific quantitative results requires caution. It is also noted that the PRC lacks a fully functional budgeting system, and there are insufficient precise statistics on the allocation of funds, such as intergovernmental fiscal transfers and local government bonds. As a result, it is difficult to accurately measure how much funding has been allocated to support achieving the dual carbon goals. This adds to the caution in interpreting the above quantitative estimation results. Nevertheless, the general conclusion drawn from the above analysis remains valid: Under the existing policy framework, the PRC faces fiscal sustainability challenges while striving to achieve the dual carbon goals.

Potential Public Financing Tools to Enhance Fiscal Sustainability

General equilibrium analyses across various country contexts consistently indicate that climate policies predominantly reliant on fiscal expenditure struggle to achieve climate goals while maintaining fiscal sustainability. Meanwhile, the PRC's dual carbon policies exhibit a heavy skew toward fiscal expenditure measures. From this perspective, it can be inferred that the existing dual carbon policies are unlikely to ensure the PRC's long-term fiscal sustainability. Furthermore, reduced-form estimation results based on the ARIMAX model also point to challenges in maintaining fiscal sustainability. In light of this situation, **expanding public financing to support the dual carbon goals is imperative for achieving fiscal sustainability**. Given this context, this section first reviews international practices in public financing for climate policy, then discusses the potential sources to enhance public financing for the PRC's dual carbon goals.

International Experience

(i) Increasing Sources of Public Financing to Support Carbon Neutrality Is a Global Issue.

In 2016, 175 parties worldwide signed the Paris Agreement, aiming to achieve peak global greenhouse gas emissions as soon as possible and carbon neutrality in the second half of this century through global cooperation. Promoting carbon neutrality has become a crucial measure for many developed and developing countries to address the climate crisis. Achieving this transition requires substantial financial support—for example, energy structure transformation, green technology research and development, and equitable safeguards—all require significant funding, undoubtedly placing enormous pressure on national finances. Simultaneously, energy structure transformation has led to a significant decline in fossil fuel-related taxes, directly impacting national revenue sources. Furthermore, energy price volatility and high inflationary pressures are continuously pushing public debt levels higher, further threatening fiscal sustainability. **According to the International Energy Agency (IEA), approximately $4.8 trillion will be needed globally by 2035 to achieve net-zero emissions, but the funding gap exceeds 65% of the total**. Of this, developed countries require approximately $195 million and developing countries $295 million, with funding gaps exceeding 50% and 70% of the required funds.[30] Traditional financing models alone are insufficient to meet such a massive financing demand. Therefore, countries around the world urgently need to explore new financing tools to ensure fiscal sustainability and provide strong support for the "carbon neutrality" transition.

[30] Calculated based on data from the International Energy Agency. 2024. *World Energy Outlook 2024*.

(ii) Carbon Pricing Is Currently the Most Important Public Financing Policy Option.

Based on international experience, carbon pricing mechanisms, green bonds, and public–private partnerships (PPPs) are widely used for climate finance. Table 10 lists the main climate policies and financing mechanisms adopted by major countries to achieve the Paris Agreement. For example, the US passed the Inflation Reduction Act in 2022, investing $369 billion to support clean energy innovation and establishing a Green Climate Fund to support low-carbon development. Its climate revenue mainly comes from the carbon market, green bonds, and PPP models. The EU implemented the Green New Deal and a carbon emissions trading system to support green economic recovery. Its main financing mechanisms are carbon market revenue and green bond issuance. As shown in Table 10, while the climate finance policies of major countries exhibit some diversity, they mainly focus

Table 10: Key Practices and Mechanisms of Climate Finance in Major Countries

Country/ Region	Key Climate Policy Initiatives	Main Financing Mechanisms
Australia	Clean Energy Finance Corporation (CEFC, $10 billion) Australian Carbon Credit Units (ACCUs) National Hydrogen Energy Strategy	Green bonds Carbon credits Preferential loans
Canada	Canada Infrastructure Bank ($35 billion) Carbon pricing system Net Zero Plan ($8 billion) Canada Green Bond Program ($3.7 billion)	Carbon tax revenue Carbon market revenue PPP Green bonds
European Union	EU Green New Deal (€1 trillion investment) EU ETS (Capital Control and Trading Mechanism) Next-generation EU plan (€750 billion for green recovery) Fair Transformation Fund	Carbon market revenue Green bonds Sustainable Finance Classification Scheme
Germany	KfW (Germany's KfW Bank invested €38 billion in 2022) Climate and Transition Fund (€177 billion) Renewable Energy Act (EEG) subsidies	State-supported financing EU green bonds Carbon market revenue
India	National Climate Change Adaptation Fund (NAFCC) Sovereign green bonds ($1 billion) FAME Program (Electric Vehicle Subsidy) International Solar Energy Union (ISA)	Government funding Carbon credit system Hybrid financing
Japan	Green Innovation Fund ($18 billion) Japan Bank for International Cooperation (JBIC) loan Asia Energy Transition Initiative ($10 billion) Tokyo Carbon Market	Preferential loans Climate Bonds
United Kingdom	UK Green Finance Strategy Sovereign green bonds (£16 billion) UK Infrastructure Bank (invested £22 billion in green investments)	Green bonds Private sector ESG funds
United States	Inflation Reduction Act ($369 billion allocated to clean energy) Green Climate Fund ($1 billion) Environmental Protection Agency (EPA) funding	Green bonds Carbon market revenue PPP

£ = pounds sterling, € = euros, ESG = environmental, social, and governance, EU = European Union, EU ETS = EU Emissions Trading System, KfW = Kreditanstalt für Wiederaufbau, PPP = public–private partnership, UK = United Kingdom.

Source: RenewConnect. 2025. Key Aspects of Climate Finance.

on three initiatives: carbon pricing, green bonds, and PPPs. Among them, green bonds and PPPs are essentially market-driven financing tools, with the government playing a guiding role; **while the carbon pricing mechanism is not only a tool for governments to achieve carbon emissions reductions, but also the most important public financing method for governments**.[31]

Carbon pricing is a mechanism that prices greenhouse gas emissions per ton of carbon dioxide equivalent, thereby internalizing the negative externalities of carbon emissions. These mechanisms include carbon taxes and emissions trading (ETS, or "carbon markets"). Since Finland introduced a nationwide carbon tax in 1990 and the EU established the world's first carbon market in 2005, an increasing number of countries have begun using carbon pricing mechanisms. As of 2024, there were 80 carbon pricing mechanisms in operation globally, including 43 carbon taxes and 35 carbon markets, covering economies representing approximately two-thirds of global GDP.[32] Table 11 shows the implementation status of carbon pricing in representative countries. Major economies that have implemented carbon taxes include France, Japan, and the UK. Separately, carbon markets have been established in jurisdictions such as Germany, the UK, and the European Union. In addition, some countries are building or about to launch carbon taxes or carbon markets; for example, India, Indonesia, and New Zealand are about to launch carbon taxes, while Albania, Brazil, and Türkiye are building carbon markets.

Since 2005, global carbon pricing revenue has increased year by year, rising from $5.8 billion in 2005 to $102.2 billion in 2024, an increase of more than 16 times (Figure 12). Compared with the $104.7 billion in carbon pricing revenue in 2023, the revenue in 2024 (68% from the carbon emissions trading market and 32% from carbon taxes) declined slightly, mainly due to the drop in emissions allowance prices in the EU carbon market (footnote 32). Nevertheless, carbon pricing revenue has remained at hundreds of billions of US dollars for 2 consecutive years (2023–2024), a scale comparable to the annual GDP of a medium-sized developing country. However, global carbon revenue is relatively concentrated in a few countries or regions. As shown in Figure 13, in 2024, 85% of global carbon revenue came from the 10 (super)countries or regions. Among them, the carbon market revenue of the EU was $41.7 billion (accounting for 41% of the total revenue), and Germany was $13.9 billion (14%).[33] The carbon tax revenue of Canada was $8.9 billion (9% of total revenue), and that of France was $7.8 billion (8% of total revenue).

[31] Although green bond issuers include governments, financial institutions, and banks, the issuance volume of green bonds by government departments is relatively low compared to nongovernment sectors.

[32] World Bank. State and Trends of Carbon Pricing Dashboard - Instrument Detail (accessed January 2026).

[33] Germany is a member of the EU and automatically participates in the EU's carbon market. In addition, Germany has its own independent carbon market, which complements the EU market and primarily covers areas not covered by the EU market, including building heating fuels and transportation fuels.

Table 11: Implementation Status of Carbon Pricing Mechanisms in Representative Countries

	Carbon Tax	Carbon Market
Albania	2008	Under investigation
Andorra	2022	
Argentina	2018	Under investigation
Austria		2022
Canada	Repealed	2019
Chile	2017	Under investigation
China, People's Republic of		2021
Colombia	2017	Under investigation
Denmark	1992	
Estonia	2000	
European Union		2005
Finland	1990	
France	2014	
Germany		2021
Hungary	2023	
Indonesia	Under investigation	2023
Israel	2025	
Japan	2012	
Republic of Korea		2015
Liechtenstein	2008	
Luxembourg	2021	
Mexico	2014	2020
Montenegro		2020
Netherlands	2021	
New Zealand	Under investigation	2008
Norway	1991	
Poland	1990	
Portugal	2015	
Singapore	2019	
Slovenia	1996	
South Africa	2019	
Spain	2014	
Sweden	1991	
Switzerland	2008	2008
Ukraine	2011	Under investigation
United Kingdom	2013	2021
Uruguay	2022	

Source: World Bank. State and Trends of Carbon Pricing Dashboard - Instrument Detail (accessed January 2026).

Figure 12: Global Carbon Pricing Revenue (2005–2024)

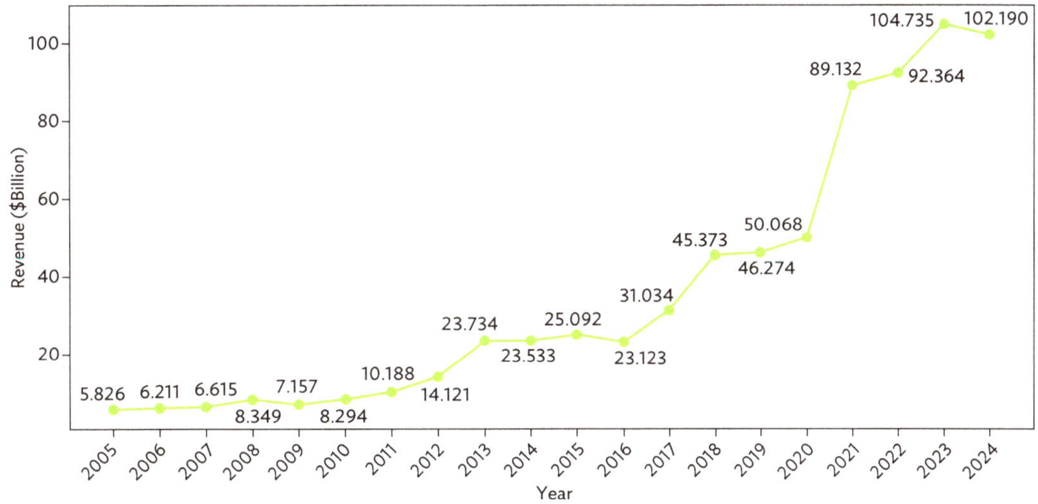

Source: World Bank. State and Trends of Carbon Pricing Dashboard - Revenue (accessed January 2026).

Figure 13: Carbon Pricing Revenue in Representative Countries or Regions (2024)

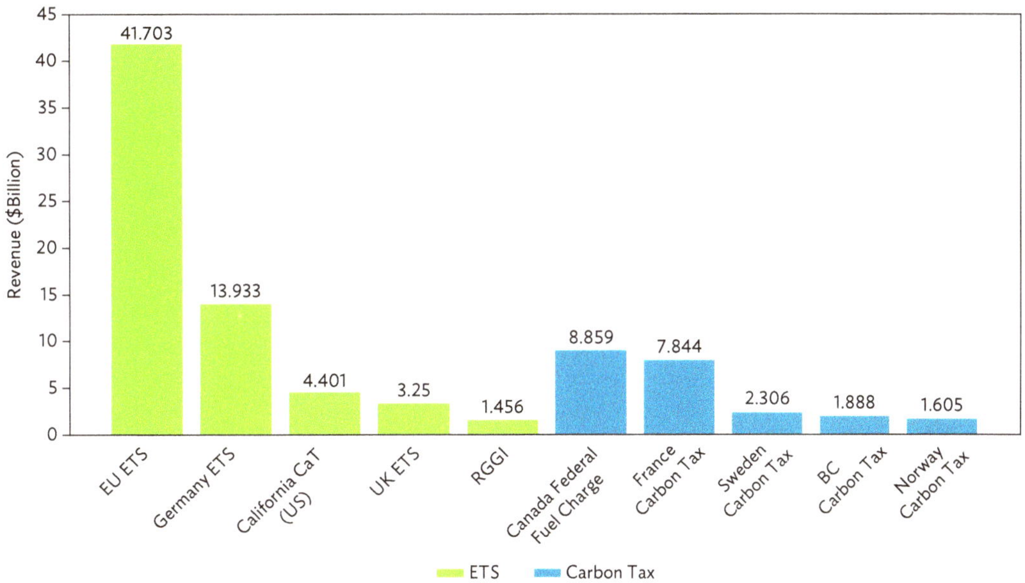

BC = British Columbia, CaT = cap and trade, ETS = emissions trading system, EU = European Union, RGGI = Regional Greenhouse Gas Initiative, UK = United Kingdom, US = United States.

Source: World Bank. State and Trends of Carbon Pricing Dashboard - Revenue (accessed January 2026).

A major driver of the rapid growth in global carbon-pricing revenue is the steady increase in global carbon prices. The average carbon price has risen from $10/ton in 2015 to $19/ton,[34] but this average price remains below the level required to achieve the Paris Agreement's temperature-control targets.[35] Meanwhile, **only 3.2% of global emissions are priced above recommended levels, and carbon prices vary significantly between countries, with the highest prices reaching 160 times the lowest** (Figure 14).[36] Specifically, carbon prices in countries such as Norway, Sweden, Switzerland, and Uruguay exceed $100/ton. Carbon prices in countries like the EU and Luxembourg are between $50/ton and $70/ton, while in countries like Kazakhstan and Mexico are less than $10/ton. The carbon pricing system generates approximately $100 billion in revenue annually. According to estimates by the Independent Panel on Climate Finance, **if all carbon emissions in 2024 were priced at $50/ton, carbon pricing tools could generate approximately $2.6 trillion in fiscal revenue.[37] Therefore, raising carbon prices would be an effective way to increase public financing for climate policy**.

Figure 14: Prices of Global Carbon Pricing Mechanism (2025)

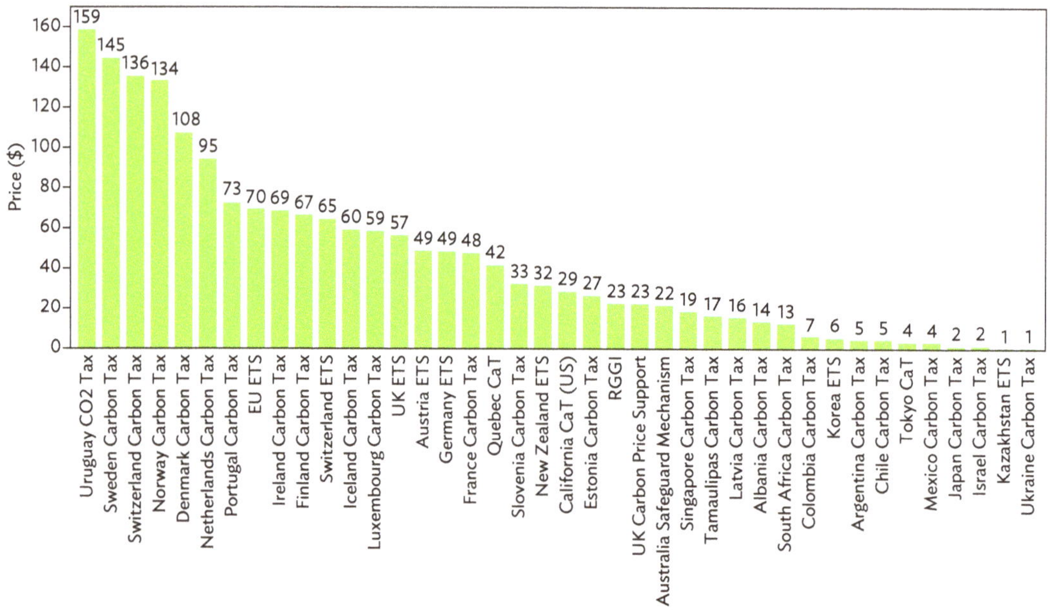

CaT = cap and trade, ETS = emissions trading system, EU = European Union, RGGI = Regional Greenhouse Gas Initiative, UK = United Kingdom, US = United States.

Source: World Bank. State and Trends of Carbon Pricing Dashboard - Revenue (accessed January 2026).

34 World Bank. 2022. *State and Trends of Carbon Pricing 2022.*

35 To achieve the goals of the Paris Agreement, the World Bank Committee recommends that carbon prices should reach $50–$100 per ton or even higher by 2030.

36 World Bank. State and Trends of Carbon Pricing Dashboard – Price (accessed January 2026)

37 G. Cayol et al. 2025. *Global Carbon Accounts 2025: Carbon pricing instruments and the unlocked potential of carbon revenues.*

Furthermore, in carbon markets, **auctions have emerged as a central mechanism for government financing**. With the exception of the PRC and the Republic of Korea—where carbon markets primarily allocate emissions allowances free of charge—most carbon markets adopt a hybrid approach combining free allocation with auctions for distributing emissions quotas. Moreover, these markets are increasingly allocating allowances through auctions.

For example: (i) The EU: As the world's largest carbon market, **57% of carbon emissions allowances in the EU carbon market are allocated through auctions**. In 2024, the EU carbon market raised €38.8 billion for the government through allowance auctions, with cumulative revenue exceeding €200 billion.[38] (ii) The US: The US has not yet formed a unified national carbon market, but has formed regional carbon markets through the Regional Greenhouse Gas Initiative (RGGI), with 91% of its allowances allocated through auctions. In 2024, the auction mechanism in the RGGI carbon market generated more than $1.5 billion in revenue, with cumulative revenue reaching $8.6 billion.[39] In addition, California has an independent carbon market, with 46% of its carbon allowances allocated through auctions, cumulatively raising $31.38 billion for the government.[40] Thus, allocating emissions allowances through auctions has great financing potential. It is estimated that allocating all carbon market allowances through auctions would generate an additional $75 billion in annual fiscal revenue.[41]

In summary, carbon pricing **is the primary public financing tool for countries seeking to achieve carbon neutrality, and its revenue is increasing year by year**. However, carbon pricing revenue still falls far short of the funds needed for global climate action. Therefore, countries worldwide are actively exploring new policy tools to increase public financing for climate policies.

(iii) Potential Public Financing Tools for the Financing Needs of Carbon Neutrality

The global climate policy financing system is mainly supported by public finance and market mechanisms, with common tools including carbon pricing mechanisms, green bonds, and PPP models. These financing tools played a crucial role in the early stages of achieving carbon neutrality. However, due to the massive scale, long duration, and high technological risks of the carbon neutrality goal, traditional financing methods are insufficient to fully address the continuously growing funding needs during the process. To overcome financing constraints, major economies such as the EU and the US are actively promoting a series of new financing initiatives.

As a core party to the Paris Agreement and an advocate for climate finance, the EU bears a significant responsibility for providing global funding for emissions reductions. However, current funding levels are insufficient to support the global goal of carbon neutrality. Therefore, in seeking new sources of fiscal funding, the EU has actively explored the following potential financing policy tools (e.g., Hirsch et al., 2023):

(a) **Fossil fuel tax. Global fossil fuel extraction levy.** Based on the "polluter pays" principle, a global tax is levied on fossil fuel extraction companies worldwide based on the carbon dioxide emissions corresponding to each barrel of oil, ton of coal, or cubic meter of

38 International Carbon Action Partnership (ICAP). EU Emissions Trading System (EU ETS) (accessed January 2026)

39 ICAP. USA - Regional Greenhouse Gas Initiative (RGGI) (accessed January 2026).

40 ICAP. USA - California Cap-and-Trade Program (accessed January 2026).

41 G. Cayol et al. 2025. *Global Carbon Accounts 2025: Carbon pricing instruments and the unlocked potential of carbon revenues.*

natural gas extracted. Many countries mainly levy resource taxes on fossil fuel extraction, such as the US mineral resources extraction tax, the UK oil and gas surcharge, and the PRC resource tax on crude oil, natural gas, and coal. However, these tax systems face many challenges and institutional deficiencies, such as the lack of a federal extraction tax in the US, the long-standing lenient fossil fuel tax system in the UK, and the relatively small size of the PRC's resource tax.[42] Therefore, implementing a unified global fossil fuel extraction tax would help fund emissions reduction and create more equal treatment. If a global fossil fuel extraction tax is implemented at a universal rate of $2 per ton of carbon dioxide, it could generate an additional $50 billion in revenue annually.[43] Increasing the tax rate would bring even more substantial fiscal revenue. In terms of specific practices, relevant countries, based on adjustments to their tax laws, transfer all or part of the revenue from fossil fuel extraction taxes to international funds, which are then distributed globally by relevant departments. However, the distribution of fossil fuels worldwide varies significantly. Therefore, support is needed for developing countries heavily reliant on energy imports; for developed countries or regions with relatively low fossil fuel production, the tax base can be expanded to include oil refining or cooking products.

(b) **Windfall profits tax on fossil fuel or solidarity levy.** Due to the surge in energy prices and corporate profits caused by the Russian invasion of Ukraine, **a one-time additional tax is levied on the unexpected excess profits gained by fossil fuel companies due to the energy crisis**. This is done to redistribute excess revenue in the energy sector and provide relief to vulnerable groups facing energy price pressures. Only a few governments levy windfall profits taxes on oil and mining companies, including EU member states such as Hungary, Italy, and Spain. In 2022, Hungary announced an 800 billion forint tax on excess profits in the financial and energy sectors over 2 years to curb inflation and fund defense spending; Italy approved an €11 billion windfall profits tax on energy companies' increased profits in 2022 to offset rising electricity, natural gas, and gasoline prices; and Spain imposed a 1.2% tax on the net income of large energy companies in 2022 to address soaring energy prices. However, windfall profits tax revenue only benefits residents and businesses affected by the energy crisis, and with energy prices fluctuating constantly, the actual tax revenue is uncertain. Therefore, the potential for using fossil fuel windfall profits taxes to support carbon neutrality goals is limited.

(c) **Shipping taxes. Air passenger levy or solidarity levy**. A differentiated surcharge levied on airfares based on ticket price, cabin class, and flight frequency, designed to raise specific funds for climate, public health, and international development. In 2006, 12 countries, including France, began collecting the air passenger levy, or solidarity levy. This differs from the fuel surcharge levied by airlines on all passengers in 2004 to offset rising international aviation fuel prices and reduce airline fuel costs, based on fuel price fluctuations. Carburant—France's airline passenger tax, or solidarity tax, is levied on business class passengers and frequent fliers under specific policies and requirements. The tax is collected by airlines and remitted to the government. It is estimated that

42 For example, some oil and gas giants in the North Sea have not paid taxes for a long time, and have even applied for tax refunds. According to the 2024 fiscal revenue and expenditure report released by the PRC's Ministry of Finance, resource tax revenue accounted for approximately 1.7% of the country's total tax revenue in 2024.

43 J.A. Richards, D. Hillman, and L. Boughey. 2019. *The Climate Damages Tax: A Guide to What It Is and How It Works.*

France's airline passenger tax generates €180 million annually, while other countries generate €22 million annually.[44] In 2008, the least developed countries proposed a national airline passenger tax, but it received little support. However, given the significant and continuously increasing carbon emissions from the global aviation industry, an airline passenger tax is imperative. In 2019, international proposals resurfaced to tax all international airline passengers based on their cabin class. In terms of potential funding, with approximately 1 billion passengers globally annually and flights growing at about 5% annually, the total revenue from airline passenger tax between 2023 and 2029 is projected to reach $8 billion–$10 billion, providing substantial funds for emissions reduction.[45]

(d) **Aviation fuel tax.** The EU Energy Taxation Directive stipulates the methods of taxing energy products and electricity, including tax reductions and exemptions for aviation and maritime fuels. The recently revised EU Energy Tax Directive stipulates that the aviation and shipping industries will no longer enjoy fuel tax exemptions, but will instead be subject to a specific tax on aircraft and marine fuel based on greenhouse gas emissions. If a shipping fuel tax is levied on all departing flights and arriving and departing ships in the future, it will bring the EU €116.4 million in revenue annually.[46] However, many emerging economies and developing countries do not support this tax.

(e) **Carbon levy on private jets and luxury yachts.** Due to inefficient energy use and highly luxurious lifestyles, private jets and luxury yachts generate significant carbon emissions. Methods for reducing carbon emissions mainly include restricting flights and navigation, levying carbon taxes, and terminating tax incentives. It is estimated that a carbon tax on private jets could raise the EU $325 million in annual revenue.[47] Portugal began levying a carbon tax on private jets in 2023, and some other EU member states have also proposed carbon taxes on private jets and luxury yachts; however, the proposed schemes vary, and it is difficult to reach consensus in the short term.

(f) **Wealth tax.** The high concentration of wealth not only exacerbates social inequality but is also closely related to high carbon emissions. **The wealth of most rich people comes from high-carbon industries**. Under the traditional industrial system, the assets of the rich come from the extraction and sale of fossil fuels; under the modern financial system, the income from the real estate, securities, and other assets of the rich is strongly correlated with the high-carbon economy. However, **the consumption behavior of the rich (such as the use of private jets, frequent long-haul air travel, high-energy-consuming facilities in their living environment, and luxury consumption) results in a significantly higher per capita carbon footprint than the social average**. A wealth tax is levied on the income from various assets and inheritance of the wealthiest individuals for a limited period. Its **impact is small, but the revenue is considerable**. Specifically,

[44] M. Wemaëre, L. Vallejo, and M. Colombier. 2023. *Financing loss and damage: Overview of tax/levy instruments under discussion.* Institute for Sustainable Development and International Relations.

[45] T. Hirsch et al. 2023. *New Sources for Public Climate Finance and for the Loss and Damage Fund* Climate Action Network (CAN) Europe.

[46] Jacob Armstrong's speech at an internal Climate Action Network Europe (CAN Europe) seminar.

[47] Council of the European Union. 2022. Council Approves 2021 Climate Finance Figure.

the EU's wealth tax affects only up to 4.8% of households, but the income can reach 10.8% of the EU's GDP.[48] It is worth noting that, to avoid wealth transfer and large-scale tax avoidance, the wealth tax should cover all forms of assets, and the supervision of "tax havens" should be strengthened.

(g) **Carbon Border Adjustment Mechanism (CBAM, also known as "carbon tariff")**. To maintain industrial competitiveness and address the risk of carbon leakage, **this mechanism prices the implicit carbon emissions generated during the production process of imported goods, ensuring that the carbon price of imported goods is comparable to that of domestically produced goods**. This mechanism applies to imported products with high carbon leakage risks, including cement, steel, and electricity. As of 2026, the EU's CBAM is in a transitional phase, covering six industries: cement, steel, aluminum, fertilizer, electricity, and hydrogen. Importers only need to declare the direct and indirect emissions of imported products, and do not need to pay the actual carbon price. On 1 January 2026, the EU officially levied the carbon tariff. Importers will purchase CBAM certificates based on the implicit carbon emissions of goods, with the price set to the weekly average auction price of quotas in the EU carbon emissions trading market. In 2030, the EU will adjust the industries covered by the carbon border adjustment mechanism. It is estimated that the carbon tariff could generate approximately €2.1 billion in annual revenue for the EU that year, but it may negatively impact developing countries.[49] Furthermore, if the revenue generated by the EU through carbon tariffs is not fully used for international climate finance, it amounts to imposing tariffs on developing countries.

(h) **Financial transaction tax**. A financial transaction tax is a tax levied on transactions involving financial instruments such as stocks, bonds, or derivatives. Since the 2008 global financial crisis, financial transaction taxes have primarily been used to raise revenue or prevent speculation. The EU first proposed a financial transaction tax in 2011, but it faced resistance from some member states. In 2013, 11 EU member states introduced a financial transaction tax through "strengthened cooperation," but failed to reach a consensus on its design. In 2019, Germany proposed a shared system of financial transaction tax revenue, but it remains under discussion. Although the financial transaction tax is not directly related to emissions reduction, its unified collection is necessary as a new source of EU self-financing, potentially bringing approximately €34 billion–€300 billion to international climate finance.[50] However, a unified collection of financial transaction taxes would also lead to competition among member states for priority in using the tax revenue.

[48] Oil Change International. 2023. *Global North leaders must redirect trillions from fossils, debt, and the 1% to address global crises.*

[49] European Union. 2021. *Proposal for a regulation of the European Parliament and of the Council establishing a carbon border adjustment mechanism.*

[50] T. Hirsch et al. 2023. *New Sources for Public Climate Finance and for the Loss and Damage Fund* Climate Action Network (CAN) Europe.

(i) **Digital services tax.** The digital services tax is levied on the total turnover derived from various digital services and applies to online advertising, digital intermediary services, and data sales. The core value of digital enterprises largely stems from user participation and data creation. Levying a digital tax ensures that enterprises' non-physical businesses provide funding for public finances, helping guide the high-quality development of the digital industry and promote industrial fairness. In 2022, the digital economy of 51 major economies worldwide reached $41.4 trillion, accounting for 46.1% of GDP.[51] Therefore, **digital services could become a source of future tax revenue. Although they cannot directly reduce carbon emissions, they can support dual carbon by opening up new tax sources**. In 2012, the OECD proposed a "two-pillar" approach to address the tax challenges of the digital economy. Before a global tax solution is reached, several jurisdictions—including EU member states such as France and Italy, as well as Kenya—have implemented or plan to implement unilateral digital services taxes as temporary measures, primarily to address profit shifting by large digital enterprises.[52] Specifically, France began levying a 3% digital services tax in 2019 on online advertising revenue and other income of companies with global annual revenue exceeding €750 million and French revenue exceeding €25 million. This tax is deductible before corporate income tax. Italy levied a 3% digital services tax in 2020 on the digital services revenue of large technology companies with global annual revenue exceeding €750 million and Italian digital services revenue exceeding €5.5 million. Kenya began levying a 1.5% digital services tax in 2020; this tax is not final but can be offset against other taxes payable by the taxpayer in that year. The European Commission estimated that a unified digital services tax could generate €5 billion in revenue for the EU in 2018.[53] Therefore, reaching a global consensus on digital taxes is necessary in the future. However, opponents argue that taxing large companies' revenue through digital services taxes is unfair, and that double taxation is difficult to avoid (Gong, 2021; Huang, Yang, and Zhang 2025).

In addition to the EU, the US has also explored several tools and options to finance climate policy, based on its own circumstances:

(a) **Vehicle miles traveled tax.** Fossil fuels are a major source of income in the US and more than a dozen other countries, directly impacting local economic growth targets, employment, and resident welfare. However, the nonrenewable nature of fossil fuels and the proposed carbon neutrality goals have led to a gradual decline in revenue from them. As an alternative to a fuel tax, **the vehicle miles traveled tax is levied based on vehicle emissions, mileage, road conditions, and other factors**. More than a dozen states in the US are piloting the vehicle-miles-traveled tax. According to calculations by the Congressional Budget Office, a tax of $0.01 per mile levied on passenger vehicles generated $28.5 billion in revenue in 2017.[54]

51 China Academy of Information and Communications Technology. 2023. *Global Digital Economy White Paper.*

52 Digital services tax is a type of income tax. Regardless of whether a digital services tax is levied, most countries follow the "place of consumption principle" and levy value-added tax on companies that provide digital services to their domestic consumers.

53 European Commission. 2017. *Communication on Fair Taxation of the Digital Economy.*

54 Government of the United States, Department of Transportation. *Highway Statistics* (accessed January 2026).

(b) **Permanent fund.** Governments invest revenues from natural resources such as coal, oil, and natural gas into permanent funds, transforming these revenues into long-term, sustainable financial assets. Investment returns are used to provide state government revenue and improve resident welfare. However, only a few states in the US have established permanent funds, including the Alaska Permanent Fund, the New Mexico Resource Tax Permanent Fund, and the Wyoming Permanent Mineral Trust Fund. Specifically, 75% of Alaska's oil extraction revenue is retained by the state government, while 25% is deposited into the Alaska Permanent Fund. This fund is managed by a state-owned fund company, with the principal used for long-term investments and investment returns distributed to residents as dividends. New Mexico's Resource Tax Permanent Fund reinvests resource extraction tax revenue, with fund income invested in general government funds to support public services such as education and health care. Wyoming invests mineral extraction revenue in a permanent mineral trust fund, with investment returns used to support the state government budget. However, amid energy shortages and the energy transition, the returns on these funds are insufficient to offset the losses from the rapid energy transition, and the scope of these revenues is relatively narrow. Therefore, future expansion of the sources and scope of use of permanent funds is essential.

(c) **Eliminate fossil fuel subsidies.** The US federal government provides $30.8 billion in subsidies to fossil fuels annually, including tax breaks and incentives, technology support subsidies, and relaxed extraction restrictions.[55] Since President Trump took office, the US has pledged an additional $4 billion in fossil fuel subsidies annually for 2025–2034. However, the US Treasury estimates that eliminating direct subsidies to fossil fuel producers could raise $35 billion over 10 years (2022–2031).[56] Therefore, eliminating fossil fuel subsidies in the future would help the transition to renewable energy and also reduce the US fiscal burden.

(d) **Levying a renewable energy tax.** For governments heavily reliant on fossil fuel taxes, clean energy offers a new potential source of revenue. According to calculations by the Montana State Revenue Department, in 2019, the department levied $9.4 million in property taxes on commercial wind power facilities based on market-value assessments.[57] However, regions heavily reliant on fossil fuel taxes may not necessarily develop clean energy. Therefore, levying a uniform renewable energy tax nationwide and distributing the revenue to states could be an important means for governments to obtain fiscal funds.

(e) **National-level carbon pricing.** The US has not yet formed a unified national carbon emissions trading system. Its carbon pricing system is primarily composed of regional carbon markets. The Regional Greenhouse Gas Initiative (RGGI) is the first carbon market-based emissions reduction system in the US. It consists of Connecticut, Delaware, Maine, Maryland, Massachusetts, New Hampshire, New Jersey, New York, Rhode Island, and Vermont. It mainly involves the thermal power generation industry.

55 Oil Change International. 2025. *Paying for Climate Chaos: US Federal Subsidies for Fossil Fuel Production.*

56 Government of the United States, Treasury Department. 2021. *General Explanations of the Administration's Fiscal Year 2022 Revenue Proposals.*

57 Montana State Taxation Bureau. *Biennial Reports* (accessed January 2026).

The government sets the total emissions cap and implements carbon quota auctions. In addition, California's carbon market implements a "cap and trade" plan that involves the power generation, petrochemical, and manufacturing industries. At the national level, there are already some proposals for carbon pricing and carbon border adjustment mechanisms. The Clean Competition Act—proposed by Democratic senators in 2022—proposed to levy carbon fees on domestic and imported products with carbon content exceeding the baseline, but it has not yet taken effect. The Foreign Pollution Fee Act, submitted in 2025, proposes classifying and taxing imported high-carbon goods based on their carbon intensity. However, due to political factors and differences in regional economic structures, implementing a unified national carbon pricing system is difficult. Nevertheless, to address climate change and insufficient government revenue, pricing carbon emissions for the entire economy will remain necessary in the future.

Policy Options for the People's Republic of China

Achieving the PRC's dual carbon goals while maintaining fiscal sustainability necessitates expanding its sources of government financing. International practices regarding climate policy financing mechanisms and new initiatives addressing the financing needs of carbon neutrality offer important references and valuable insights for the PRC to develop additional public financing policy options to achieve its dual carbon goals. As the world's largest developing country and carbon emitter, the PRC should, based on extensive international experience, construct a multitiered, systematic, and uniquely Chinese dual carbon public financing mechanism.

(i) Short-Term Policy Options

In the short term, policy options could consider implementing incremental reforms within the existing institutional framework and policy architecture to minimize resistance and challenges. Specifically:

(a) **Leveraging the financing function of the carbon market. Achieving a shift from free allowances to paid auctions.** The allocation method of carbon market allowances is a key link in the carbon market and a core element in leveraging its financing function. From international experience, **carbon markets in the EU, the US, and other countries have generated substantial fiscal revenue for governments through auctions of carbon allowances. In 2024, the EU carbon market raised €38.8 billion for the government through auction mechanisms, with cumulative revenue from allowance auctions exceeding €200 billion;** California's carbon market has raised $31.38 billion for the government. The PRC's carbon market officially began trading in July 2021. Prior to this, eight provinces and municipalities, including Beijing, Chongqing, Shanghai, and Tianjin, had conducted carbon market pilot programs since 2013. Taking Beijing as an example, its carbon market introduced an auction mechanism in 2022, with an annual auction rate not exceeding 5%, generating a cumulative revenue of CNY319 million. However, while the national carbon market has reduced carbon emissions through the free allocation of carbon allowances, it has not made a significant contribution to climate finance. Therefore, in May 2025, the General Office of the CPC Central Committee and the General Office of the State Council issued the Opinions on Promoting Green and Low-Carbon Transformation and Strengthening the Construction of the National

Carbon Market (the "Opinions"), which pointed out that by 2030, the goal is to establish a "national carbon emission trading market that combines free and paid allocation." Drawing on international experience, domestic pilot experiences, and relevant opinions, the PRC can gradually introduce an auction mechanism in the short term. Regarding auction policies, policies and rules should be improved for auction participants, auction frequency, timing, triggering mechanisms, and auction risk management (Qi, 2024). Regarding auction ratios, when allocating carbon quotas, the auction mechanism should be introduced gradually, initially using a lower proportion of auction quotas, and then gradually increasing the proportion of quotas auctioned for payment each year. Regarding auction prices, a price stabilization mechanism should be established, along with a reserve price for auctions and a quota reserve system.

(b) **Expanding the industry coverage of the carbon market.** The EU's carbon market covers industries such as power, steel, cement, ceramics, shipping, and maritime transport, and plans to include construction and road transport, and municipal waste incineration by 2026. In contrast, the PRC's carbon market only includes industries such as power, steel, cement, and aluminum smelting, covering approximately 60% of the country's total carbon dioxide emissions. Furthermore, carbon markets in Beijing, Shanghai, and Shenzhen include the transportation industry within their scope, while those in Fujian, Guangdong, and Tianjin include the civil aviation sector. **Compared with mature carbon markets worldwide, the PRC's carbon market covers far fewer industries.** The 2025 Opinions document states that by 2027, "the national carbon emissions trading market will basically cover major emitting industries in the industry sector, and the national voluntary greenhouse gas emissions reduction trading market will achieve full coverage of key areas." Therefore, the PRC can systematically expand the scope of covered industries based on industry development status, carbon reduction and pollution control contributions, data quality, and carbon emissions characteristics. Specifically, in the short term, the plan will further include industries such as building materials, non-ferrous metals, chemicals, papermaking, and aviation in the national carbon market, supplemented by an auction mechanism, to provide sustainable financial support for achieving the dual carbon goals.

(c) **Increasing carbon trading prices.** In 2024, the PRC's average carbon price was CNY91.8/ton, about twice the price at the beginning of the market launch (K. Wang and C. Lü. 2025). However, the PRC's carbon price level still lags those of mature carbon markets. Carbon prices in countries such as Luxembourg and the EU range from $50/ton to $70/ton. Carbon prices are closely related to carbon emissions quotas. Two methods are commonly used worldwide for quota allocation: one based on the total emissions-reduction target, and the other on emissions intensity. Most carbon markets use targets, such as the EU and the Republic of Korea. Due to the failure to achieve a carbon peak and limited market flexibility in related industries, the PRC uses an emissions-intensity-based quota system. However, this method is prone to excessively high carbon quotas due to overly lenient baseline standards, which in turn lead to persistently low carbon prices. In August 2024, the State Council issued the Work Plan for Accelerating the Construction of a Dual Carbon Emission Control System, which proposed that the PRC would implement a dual carbon emissions control system from 2026 to 2030, with intensity control as the main focus and total emissions control as a supplement, and then gradually shift to total emissions control as the main focus. The Opinions issued in 2025 further stated that by 2030, a national carbon emissions trading market based on quota control would be basically established. By controlling total emissions and gradually increasing carbon trading prices, it is beneficial to provide financial support for achieving emissions-reduction targets while advancing dual carbon goals.

(d) **Reducing fiscal subsidies for fossil fuel-related industries.** Fossil fuel subsidies are fiscal subsidy policies implemented by governments to support the development of fossil fuel-related industries (such as coal, oil, and natural gas), including explicit and implicit subsidies. According to IMF estimates (Figure 15), from 2015 to 2022, the scale of the PRC's government subsidies for fossil fuels continued to rise. In 2015, the total subsidy scale reached $1.206 trillion, of which implicit subsidies amounted to $1.191 trillion. **In 2022, the PRC's subsidies for fossil fuels increased to $2.235 trillion, accounting for 12.5% of the national GDP that year, of which implicit subsidies totaled as much as $1.960 trillion.**

Figure 15: Size of Chinese Government Subsidies for Fossil Energy (2015–2022)

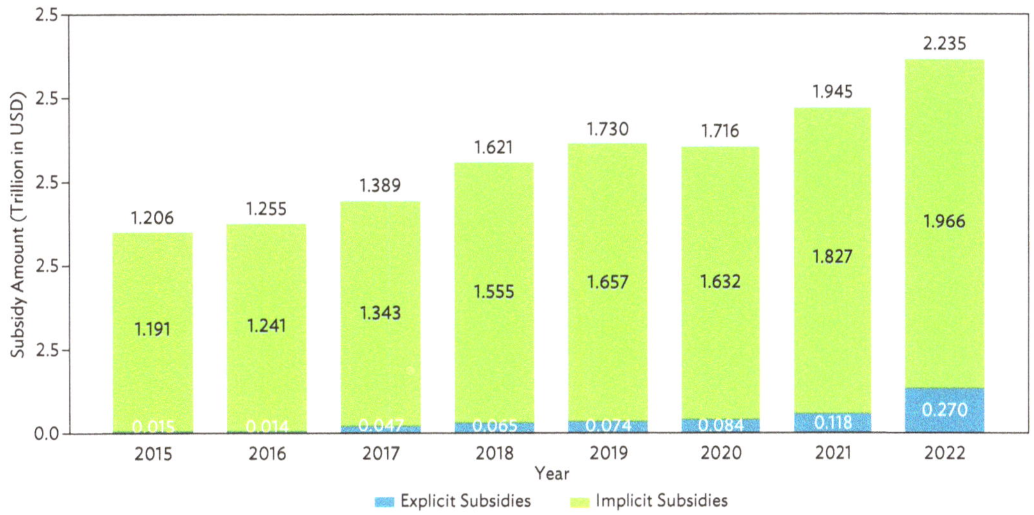

Source: International Monetary Fund. IMF Fossil Energy Subsidies Database (accessed January 2026).

Such a massive scale of subsidies has resulted in a significant fiscal burden, crowding out fiscal spending in crucial areas such as healthcare, education, and green investment. Therefore, by eliminating tax incentives for relevant industries and implementing differentiated tax and fee reduction policies, more potential funds can be released for the dual carbon goals while reducing fiscal expenditure. **First, consider eliminating subsidies for fossil fuel-related industries:** (i) For the electricity and heating sector, consider eliminating the exemption of land use tax for thermal power plants and the exemption of value-added tax (VAT) and property tax for heating companies. (ii) For the transport sector, consider eliminating fuel subsidies for professional fuel users (such as taxi drivers). (iii) For the product consumption sector, eliminate the "floor price" protection mechanism for refined oil products and the preferential VAT rates for fossil fuel products such as coal, gas, and liquefied petroleum gas. **Second, implementing differentiated tax and fee reduction policies.** Since 2019, the PRC has implemented larger-scale tax and fee reductions, explicitly reducing the VAT for manufacturing from 16% to 13%, and for transport and construction from 10% to 9%. However, these industries involve energy-intensive and high-emissions enterprises. Therefore, for industries with high carbon emissions, future tax and fee reductions should be implemented to alleviate carbon emissions while increasing fiscal sustainability.

(e) **Expanding the existing green tax system.** The PRC has established a green tax system primarily composed of the Environmental Protection Tax, supplemented by the Resource Tax, Consumption Tax, and the Vehicle and Vessel Tax. From 2009 to 2022, the PRC's green tax revenue increased from CNY5.95 trillion to CNY16.66 trillion, and its share of total tax revenue also increased year by year. However, overall, the **proportion of green tax revenue is still relatively low, accounting for only 13.62% in 2022 (Table 12). Therefore, to improve financial support for achieving the dual carbon goals, it is imperative to expand the existing green tax system.**

Table 12: Green Tax Revenue in the People's Republic of China (2009–2022) (CNY100 million)

Years	Environmental Protection Tax	Resource Tax	Consumption Tax	Vehicle Purchase Tax	Vehicle and Vessel Tax	Green Tax Total	Tax Revenue	Green Tax Percentage (%)
2009	173	338	4,761	1,164	187	6,623	59,522	11.13
2010	188	418	6,072	1,793	242	8,712	73,211	11.90
2011	190	596	6,936	2,045	302	10,069	89,739	11.22
2012	189	904	7,876	2,229	393	11,591	100,614	11.52
2013	205	1,006	8,231	2,596	474	12,512	110,531	11.32
2014	187	1,084	8,907	2,885	541	13,604	119,175	11.42
2015	179	1,035	10,542	2,793	613	15,161	124,922	12.14
2016	210	951	10,217	2,674	683	14,735	130,361	11.30
2017	218	1,353	10,225	3,281	774	15,850	144,370	10.98
2018	206	1,630	10,632	3,453	831	16,751	156,403	10.71
2019	213	1,822	12,564	3,498	881	18,978	157,992	12.01
2020	200	1,755	12,028	3,531	945	18,459	136,780	13.50
2021	203	2,288	13,881	3,520	1,021	20,913	172,731	12.11
2022	211	3,389	16,699	2,398	1,039	22,697	166,614	13.62

CNY = Chinese renminbi (yuan).

Source: Government of the People's Republic of China, China Finance Yearbook Editorial Committee. Fiscal Yearbook 2010–2023. China State Finance Magazine Agency.

(f) **Resource tax reform.** The PRC levies resource taxes on fossil fuels such as crude oil, natural gas, and coal, but the overall scale is relatively small. Statistics show that in 2024, energy tax revenue accounted for 4.1% of Germany's total tax revenue,[58] and natural resource use tax revenue accounted for 13.8% of the Russian Federation's total tax revenue.[59] In contrast, the PRC's resource tax revenue was projected to account for only 1.7% of its total tax revenue in 2025.[60] Therefore, deepening resource tax reform is necessary. **First, increasing the resource tax rate for coal.** The PRC levies a 6% resource tax on crude oil and natural gas, and a tax rate ranging from 2% to 10% on coal, with the specific rate determined by each province and city. In reality, most provinces have adopted a lower rate (Hao, 2025). In 2020, coal accounted for 66% of total carbon emissions from the energy system (Xu, 2018), far exceeding those of oil and natural gas. Therefore, to increase future resource tax revenue, the minimum statutory resource tax rate for coal should be set as a priority. **Second, expanding the scope of resource tax collection.** The PRC's resource tax covers energy minerals, metallic minerals, nonmetallic minerals, water and gas minerals, and salt, with limited coverage. Therefore, it is advisable to consider including the future development and/or use of ecological resources such as forests and wetlands within the scope of resource tax collection, thereby protecting carbon sink resources while expanding the tax base (Chen, Wang, and Dai 2025; Xie 2025; Zhang 2025).

(g) **Gradually increasing the statutory tax rate for the environmental protection tax.** The PRC's environmental protection tax operates on a range-based rate system, with the specific tax amount determined by each province. To promote economic development, more than one-third of the provinces nationwide use the statutory minimum tax rate (Hao, 2025). Therefore, increasing the statutory tax rate for environmental protection tax in the future will, to some extent, increase local government revenue and promote low-carbon transformation.

(h) **Appropriately expanding the tax base for the consumption tax on fuel energy.** Countries like Canada and the US levy consumption taxes on petroleum products, solid fuels, and gaseous fuels, but the PRC only levies a consumption tax on refined oil products. In the future, the PRC could further expand the scope of its fossil fuel consumption tax, explicitly extending the tax base to petroleum products used for fuel and power (including other solid and gaseous fuels and refined oil products) (Hao, 2025). Furthermore, the PRC's constraints on high-carbon products are insufficient; highly polluting products such as plastic packaging and chemical pesticides are not yet included in the consumption tax scope (Chen, 2025). Therefore, in the future, highly polluting products such as plastic packaging could be included in the scope of the consumption tax to promote low-carbon transformation at the consumption end and raise more funds for emissions reduction efforts.

58 Census and Economic Information Center (CEIC). Government of Germany Tax Revenue: Federal: Energy (2006–2026) (accessed January 2026).

59 Census and Economic Information Center Database (accessed January 2026).

60 The PRC's Ministry of Finance released its 2025 fiscal revenue and expenditure report.

(ii) Long-Term Policy Options

In the long term, policy options will require structural reforms within the existing institutional framework and policy system, with the introduction of taxes aimed at achieving the dual carbon goals serving as the primary direction of reform. Specifically:

(a) **Imposing a carbon tax.** The PRC has initially established a national carbon emissions trading market. However, challenges such as inconsistent carbon emissions monitoring and verification standards, limited industry coverage (unsuitable for point-source pollution industries), and relatively low carbon prices have constrained its effectiveness in incentivizing emissions reduction behaviors. **The introduction of a carbon tax could serve as a complementary measure to address these limitations.** From the perspective of the PRC's tax system structure, it is possible to consider setting the carbon tax under the environmental protection tax framework, and gradually build a carbon tax and carbon market integration mechanism with Chinese characteristics through pilot projects followed by expansion (e.g., pilot projects in industries with large carbon emissions, urgent emissions reduction needs, and high carbon emissions data quality), differentiated tax rate design (e.g., taxing at a lower tax rate in the initial stage and then gradually increasing it dynamically), and tax incentives (e.g., exempting or reducing carbon tax for industries such as electricity, steel, and cement that have already been included in the carbon market, reducing or exempting part of the carbon tax for enterprises that adopt emissions reduction technologies, and temporarily not taxing carbon emissions from personal life). However, before levying a carbon tax, it is crucial to fully consider its impact on the operating costs and international competitiveness of relevant industries, the effects of rising energy prices on low-income groups, and the coordination between the carbon tax and other policies to avoid double taxation. In particular, **the coordination between the carbon tax and the carbon market is the cornerstone of building a complete carbon pricing system.** Internationally, carbon pricing mechanisms are mainly divided into two models: complementary and overlapping. Complementary carbon pricing treats the carbon tax as a supplement to the carbon market, levying a carbon tax on enterprises or sectors not included in the carbon trading system (such as France, Iceland, and Ireland); overlapping carbon pricing implements dual regulation of the same emissions source within the coverage of the carbon market and the carbon tax (such as Mexico, the Netherlands, Poland, Sweden, and the UK). Comparatively, **the complementary carbon pricing mechanism faces less resistance and cost, making it suitable for the initial stages of policy implementation; while the overlapping carbon pricing mechanism has a greater emissions-reduction effect and is suitable for policy environments with stricter standards.** Considering the PRC's national conditions, in the medium to long term, the PRC can steadily promote a complementary carbon pricing mechanism; in the long term, it can explore transitional schemes to an overlapping carbon pricing mechanism.

(b) **Introducing a carbon border adjustment mechanism ("carbon tariff").** The PRC has not levied an independent carbon tariff, but as a measure to address the risk of carbon spillover, it can serve the country's dual carbon strategy by pricing the implicit carbon emissions generated during the production process of imported products, as well as preventing domestic enterprises that strictly implement emissions reduction requirements from being at a disadvantage in international competition. In the future, the PRC can integrate the carbon tariff into the existing import consumption tax, following the principle of gradual implementation, prioritizing pilot implementation in high-carbon industries such as steel, cement, and fertilizer, and then gradually expanding the scope; establish a carbon footprint monitoring and accounting system for imported products using the carbon emissions during their production process and even throughout their entire life cycle as the basis for taxation; and link it with the carbon tax and the domestic carbon market, formulating a reasonable tax rate with reference to domestic carbon prices and quota methods.

(c) **Imposing aviation-related taxes.** Compared with high-carbon industries such as electricity, steel, and chemicals, the PRC's aviation industry has relatively low carbon emissions, but its potential for carbon emissions growth is large, and reducing emissions is difficult. Domestic airlines are reducing aviation carbon emissions by using sustainable aviation fuels and other measures, but due to cost constraints, the large-scale promotion of sustainable aviation fuels poses significant challenges. Therefore, levying air passenger taxes and aviation fuel taxes may be a feasible approach. **Levying air passenger taxes.** To cope with fluctuations in aviation fuel prices, airlines charge all passengers an additional fuel surcharge based on the route distance. The fuel surcharge for routes over 800 kilometers is CNY40, and the fuel surcharge for routes under 800 kilometers is CNY20. In 2006, airlines in 12 countries, including France, began levying air passenger taxes on business-class passengers and frequent flyers. The revenue raised was handed over to the government, which then raised substantial funds for climate, public health, and other causes in various countries. There are about 1 billion passengers worldwide each year, and flights grow by about 5% annually. If an air passenger tax is levied, it could raise $8 billion–$10 billion in revenue over the next 6 years (2023-2028).[61] Therefore, **in the future, in addition to the fuel surcharge airlines levy, the PRC could levy an aviation passenger tax on business class passengers and frequent flyers.** The airlines would collect this tax and remit it to the government, providing financial support for achieving the dual carbon (carbon and carbon emissions) target. **An aviation fuel tax could be levied.** Although the PRC reinstated VAT on aviation fuel in 2013, including VAT on aviation fuel within the deductible scope did not significantly change the overall tax burden on airlines. In the future, levying a specific tax on aircraft fuel based on greenhouse gas emissions would help reduce emissions and raise funds to support the dual carbon goals.

(d) **Imposing a wealth tax on the rich.** The PRC faces a significant wealth gap, with the Gini coefficient exceeding the international warning line.[62] Besides income inequality, the PRC also suffers from high wealth concentration, with 1.0% of households controlling more than 30.0% of the nation's wealth. By 2025, fewer than 0.5% of households nationwide will possess net assets of tens of millions of yuan, and the generation and consumption of this wealth are closely linked to high carbon emissions.[63] Therefore, **targeting a small**

[61] T. Hirsch et al. 2023. *New Sources for Public Climate Finance and for the Loss and Damage Fund* Climate Action Network (CAN) Europe.

[62] J. Li et al. 2015. *Report on the Development of People's Livelihood in the PRC* [M]. Peking University Press. 201511(216).

[63] Hurun Report. 2025. *2024 Hurun Wealth Report*.

number of high-asset groups for taxation would help narrow the wealth gap and generate substantial fiscal revenue, contributing to emissions-reduction goals. This characteristic provides a realistic feasibility for levying a wealth tax on the rich. The PRC could adopt a progressive wealth tax, levying taxes on income from various assets and on inheritances of the wealthiest individuals within a limited period. The tax base should cover all asset forms, and supervision of tax havens should be strengthened to prevent wealth transfer and large-scale tax evasion.

(e) **Imposing a vehicle mileage tax.** Regarding highway taxes and fees, the PRC mainly levies consumption taxes, such as the vehicle purchase tax and the vehicle fuel tax. In achieving the dual carbon goal, new energy vehicles are gradually replacing fuel vehicles, and the traditional vehicle tax base based on fuel consumption is shrinking, making it difficult to fund the low-carbon transformation. Hainan Province in the PRC has launched a pilot reform of highway mileage fees, adhering to the principle of "accurate payment by road users," and using satellite navigation systems to implement differentiated charges based on mileage, road grade, vehicle type, and emission type. **The vehicle mileage tax is a tax distinct from vehicle purchase tax, vehicle fuel tax, and consumption tax; it is a new tax levied on vehicle ownership, use, and near-consumption stages based on vehicle mileage.** In the future, the vehicle mileage tax levy should consider its synergistic relationship with existing vehicle purchase tax, vehicle fuel tax, and vehicle toll fees. Vehicle purchase tax is used for the construction and maintenance of transportation infrastructure and can coexist with vehicle mileage tax; to reduce the tax burden on users, **vehicle fuel tax can be replaced by vehicle mileage tax in the future;** vehicle toll is a type of mileage fee, and with the use of navigation systems for precise positioning, it is worth considering merging vehicle mileage tax and vehicle toll.

(f) **Promoting digital service tax.** In 2023, the PRC's digital economy reached CNY53.9 trillion, accounting for 42.8% of GDP.[64] This means that in the future, the PRC's digital services tax collection can serve as an important source of tax revenue for the national treasury and help fund the dual carbon goal. The PRC mainly levies VAT on most digital services and has tax exemption policies for specific situations. For general taxpayers of digital services such as cloud services, online advertising, and software services, the tax rate is 6%; small-scale taxpayers are subject to a tax rate of 3%; and digital services provided to overseas entities and consumed entirely overseas are exempt from VAT. However, under the tax system, digital services are taxed under the principle of place of production, resulting in significant tax losses in the place of consumption. Moreover, digital service enterprises have no physical presence, and if they do not actively declare it, it is difficult to determine their tax jurisdiction. To actively follow the OECD's "dual pillar" international tax scheme, the PRC may choose between two approaches to taxing digital services in the future. **One is to implement a consumption-based tax principle for digital services.** VAT is levied when consumers complete their purchases. Digital service companies collect and remit the tax to a dedicated VAT account for digital services, providing the tax authorities with information on the place of consumption. Finally, the tax authorities refund the tax to the place of consumption (Wang and Xu, 2021). **The other**

[64] China Academy of Information and Communications Technology. 2024. *China Digital Economy Development Research Report 2024*.

is to levy an independent digital services tax. The PRC has not yet introduced a digital tax to address profit shifting by large enterprises. Therefore, the PRC may need to develop a digital services tax similar to those in EU countries in the future. The tax base for digital services taxes abroad is digital service revenue. Drawing on international experience, the PRC could set the tax base for its digital services tax as digital service revenue minus calculable costs, and levy it at an appropriate tax rate.

Concluding Remarks

Faced with the increasingly severe global climate crisis, 178 parties signed the Paris Agreement in 2016, aiming to achieve global carbon peaking and carbon neutrality. As the largest developing country and carbon emitter, the PRC proposed the dual carbon goals in 2020: peaking carbon before 2030 and achieving carbon neutrality before 2060. In implementing related work, fiscal policy has provided a solid guarantee for the green and low-carbon transformation of the economy and society through financial support, tax incentives, and green government procurement. However, the sustainable development of fiscal policy also faces significant challenges. Therefore, this report, based on a review of the dual carbon implementation plan, summarizes the current fiscal and tax policies supporting the dual carbon goals, analyzes their impact on fiscal sustainability, and explores potential financing tools to enhance the PRC's fiscal sustainability, drawing on international experience.

To ensure the timely achievement of the dual carbon goals, the PRC has established a 1+N policy system guided by the Working Opinions and the Action Plan. This system clarifies the quantitative targets and specific action road maps for dual carbon work at three key time nodes: 2025, 2030, and 2060. It also formulates specific implementation plans and supporting measures covering key areas and industries. Guided by this top-level institutional design, various sectors and provinces have collaborated to implement precise policies, maintaining a high degree of consistency with the national strategy in overall objectives while selecting tailored, phased quantitative targets and implementation paths that align with their industry characteristics and regional resource endowments. This has ensured the steady progress and effective implementation of dual carbon work nationwide.

As a foundation and crucial pillar of national governance, public finance plays a vital supporting role in implementing the dual carbon goals. The PRC has established a relatively systematic and comprehensive fiscal and tax policy framework, organically combining three major policy tools—fiscal expenditure, tax incentives and/or constraints, and market guidance—to facilitate the green and low-carbon transformation of the economy and society. Specifically, in terms of expenditure policy, a series of special funds established by the government provide targeted support for energy transition and industry emissions reduction; fiscal subsidies directly reduce consumer costs; and green government procurement, by prioritizing the purchase of energy-saving and environmentally friendly products, plays a demand-leading role, driving the green upgrading of the industrial chain. In terms of tax policy, incentive and constraint policies work in tandem. Tax incentives encourage enterprises to engage in energy conservation, environmental protection, and comprehensive resource utilization; while resource taxes and environmental protection taxes increase the cost of using fossil fuels, curbing high-carbon behavior. However, the tax system is insufficient in its financing function for achieving the dual carbon goals, lacking a carbon pricing tool that directly taxes carbon emissions, thus restricting its fundraising capacity. At the same time, the policy system, dominated by fiscal expenditure, further increases the fiscal burden.

From a short-term perspective, this report's estimates indicate that the total funds required to achieve the dual carbon goals are extremely large. There remains a significant gap between dual carbon fiscal expenditures and the required fiscal funds, with pronounced regional differences, particularly in Inner Mongolia, Ningxia, Shanxi, and Xinjiang. From a medium- to long-term perspective, this report—which combines previous literature using dynamic and/or computable general equilibrium models to estimate the impact of climate policies in other countries and regions—discusses the impact of the PRC's dual carbon policy on fiscal sustainability. A reduced-form model is used to predict the fiscal sustainability of the entire country and of representative provinces as the country achieves the carbon peak. The basic conclusions of the study are adopting a carbon neutrality policy dominated by fiscal expenditure will lead to a significant increase in government debt ratios, making it difficult to achieve sustainable fiscal development; adopting a reasonable combination of revenue and expenditure policies, including carbon taxes, is conducive to maintaining fiscal sustainability; and finally, the PRC's achievement of the carbon neutrality target and maintenance of fiscal sustainability will inevitably require the support of additional revenue-generating fiscal instruments.

Increasing public financing for dual carbon goals has become an inevitable requirement for achieving fiscal sustainability. Carbon pricing is the primary fiscal financing tool for major countries worldwide. However, carbon pricing revenue still falls far short of the funds needed for global climate action. Therefore, countries around the world are actively exploring policy tools to increase public financing for climate policies. Internationally, the EU has focused on new tax tools such as levies on fossil fuel profiteering, air passenger taxes, wealth taxes, and carbon tariffs; the US has discussed financing tools such as vehicle mileage taxes, expanded permanent funds, and renewable energy taxes. These practices and policy discussions provide diverse references for the PRC in addressing the fiscal sustainability issues in achieving its dual carbon goals. Based on international experience and the PRC's national conditions, the PRC needs to build a multitiered financing mechanism, with short-term policies focusing on optimizing existing tools. First, activating the financing function of the carbon market, gradually shifting from free allowances to paid auctions, expanding the industry coverage of the carbon market, and appropriately increasing carbon prices. Second, reducing subsidies for the fossil fuel industry and differentiating the intensity of tax and fee reductions for high-carbon industries. Third, expanding the existing green tax system by deepening resource tax reform, levying air passenger and fuel taxes, raising the statutory tax rate for environmental protection taxes, and expanding the tax base for consumption taxes.

In the long term, the PRC should explore new public financing tools. (i) Under the framework of environmental protection taxes, a carbon tax could be considered for introduction at an appropriate time, gradually building a carbon tax and carbon market integration mechanism with Chinese characteristics. (ii) Introducing a carbon tariff, prioritizing pilot programs in high-carbon industries such as steel and cement, and establishing a carbon footprint accounting system for imported products. (iii) Levying aviation-related taxes. (iv) Levying a progressive wealth tax for the wealthy. (v) Promoting a vehicle mileage tax and coordinating its relationship with existing vehicle taxes and fees. (vi) Prudently advancing a digital service tax, exploring the principle of taxation at the place of consumption, or introducing an independent tax. In summary, the PRC should build a dual carbon public financing system with Chinese characteristics by combining "short-term optimization of existing tools and long-term policy innovation." This will alleviate fiscal pressures and also contribute to the PRC's solutions to global climate governance.

Appendix

Table A1: Implementation Plans for Carbon Peaking in Different Provinces

Provinces and Cities	Policy Documents
Beijing	• Beijing's Carbon Peak Implementation Plan (2022)
Tianjin	• Carbon Peak Implementation Plan (2022) • Tianjin Municipality's 2022 Implementation Plan for Science and Technology Support to Achieve Carbon Peak and Carbon Neutrality • Tianjin Municipality's 2022 Implementation Plan for Synergistic Efficiency Improvement in Pollution Reduction and Carbon Reduction
Hebei Province	• 2022 Hebei Province Carbon Peak Implementation Plan • 2023 Hebei Province Industrial Sector Carbon Peak Implementation Plan • 2023 Hebei Province Urban and Rural Construction Carbon Peak Implementation Plan
Shanxi Province	• Carbon Peak Implementation Plan (2023) • 2023 Implementation Plan for Carbon Peaking in Urban and Rural Construction in Shanxi Province
Inner Mongolia Autonomous Region	• 2022 Inner Mongolia Autonomous Region Carbon Peak Implementation Plan • 2023 Inner Mongolia Autonomous Region Industrial Sector Carbon Peak Implementation Plan • 2024 Inner Mongolia Autonomous Region Carbon Peak Pilot Construction Plan
Liaoning Province	• Liaoning Province Carbon Peak Implementation Plan (2022) • Liaoning Province's 2023 Implementation Plan for Science and Technology Support to Achieve Carbon Peak and Carbon Neutrality
Jilin Province	• Jilin Province Carbon Peak Implementation Plan (2022) • Jilin Province's 14th Five-Year Plan for Waste-Free City Construction (2023)
Heilongjiang Province	• 2022 Heilongjiang Province Carbon Peak Implementation Plan • 2022 Heilongjiang Province Industrial Sector Carbon Peak Implementation Plan • 2022 Heilongjiang Province Urban and Rural Construction Carbon Peak Implementation Plan
Shanghai	• Carbon Peak Implementation Plan (2022) • Shanghai's 2022 Implementation Plan for Carbon Peaking in Urban and Rural Construction • Implementation Opinions of Shanghai Municipality on Providing Fiscal Support for Achieving Carbon Peaking and Carbon Neutrality in 2023
Jiangsu Province	• Jiangsu Province's 2023 Implementation Plan for Carbon Peaking in Urban and Rural Construction
Zhejiang Province	• 2023 Zhejiang Province Industrial Sector Carbon Peak Implementation Plan • 2021 Zhejiang Province Carbon Peak and Carbon Neutrality Technological Innovation Action Plan
Anhui Province	• Anhui Province Carbon Peak Implementation Plan (2022) • 2022 Anhui Province Urban and Rural Construction Carbon Peak Implementation Plan
Fujian Province	• 2022 Implementation Opinions on Fully and Accurately Implementing the New Development Philosophy and Doing a Good Job in Carbon Peaking and Carbon Neutrality • 2023 Fujian Province Urban and Rural Construction Carbon Peak Implementation Plan • 2023 Fujian Province Industrial Sector Carbon Peak Implementation Plan

continued on next page

Table A1 *continued*

Provinces and Cities	Policy Documents
Jiangxi Province	• 2022 Jiangxi Province Carbon Peak Implementation Plan • 2022 Implementation Plan for Carbon Peaking in Urban and Rural Construction in Jiangxi Province
Shandong Province	• Shandong Province Carbon Peak Implementation Plan (2022) • 2023 Shandong Province Urban and Rural Construction Carbon Peak Implementation Plan
Henan Province	• 2023 Henan Province Carbon Peak Implementation Plan
Hubei Province	• 2023 Hubei Province Urban and Rural Construction Carbon Peak Implementation Plan • Hubei Province's 2022 Action Plan for Technological Innovation to Achieve Carbon Peak and Carbon Neutrality
Hunan Province	• Hunan Province Carbon Peak Implementation Plan (2022) • 2025 Implementation Plan for Carbon Peaking in Urban and Rural Construction in Hunan Province
Guangdong Province	• Guangdong Province Carbon Peak Implementation Plan (2022) • Guangdong Province's 2023 Implementation Plan for Synergistic Efficiency Improvement in Pollution Reduction and Carbon Reduction
Guangxi Zhuang Autonomous Region	• 2022 Guangxi Zhuang Autonomous Region Carbon Peak Implementation Plan
Hainan Province	• Hainan Province Carbon Peak Implementation Plan (2022) • Hainan Province's Three-Year Action Plan for the Development and Upgrading of Prefabricated Buildings (Green Buildings) (2023–2025)
Chongqing	• Chongqing Municipality's 2023 Implementation Plan for Carbon Peaking in the Industrial Sector • Chongqing Municipality's 2023 Implementation Plan for Carbon Peaking in Urban and Rural Construction
Sichuan Province	• 2022 Sichuan Province Carbon Peak Implementation Plan • 2022 Sichuan Province Energy Sector Carbon Peak Implementation Plan
Guizhou Province	• Guizhou Province Carbon Peak Implementation Plan (2022) • 2023 Guizhou Province Urban and Rural Construction Carbon Peak Implementation Plan • 2023 Guizhou Province Pollution Reduction and Carbon Reduction Synergistic Efficiency Enhancement Implementation Plan
Yunnan Province	• Yunnan Province Carbon Peak Implementation Plan (2022)
Tibet Autonomous Region	• 2023 Implementation Plan for Carbon Peaking in the Industrial Sector of Tibet Autonomous Region
Shaanxi Province	• 2022 Shaanxi Province Carbon Peak Implementation Plan • 2023 Implementation Plan for Carbon Peaking in Shaanxi Province's Industrial Sector
Gansu Province	• Gansu Province Carbon Peak Implementation Plan (2023)
Qinghai Province	• 2022 Qinghai Province Carbon Peak Implementation Plan • 2023 Qinghai Province Industrial Sector Carbon Peak Implementation Plan • 2023 Qinghai Province Urban and Rural Construction Carbon Peak Implementation Plan
Ningxia Hui Autonomous Region	• 2022 Ningxia Hui Autonomous Region Carbon Peak Implementation Plan • 2022 Ningxia Hui Autonomous Region Urban and Rural Construction Carbon Peak Implementation Plan • Implementation Plan for Key Tasks of Ningxia Hui Autonomous Region in Accelerating the Construction of a Dual Carbon Emission Control System (2024)
Xinjiang Uygur Autonomous Region	• 2023 Xinjiang Uygur Autonomous Region Carbon Peak Implementation Plan • 2023 Implementation Plan for Carbon Peaking in the Industrial Sector of Xinjiang Uygur Autonomous Region • 2023 Implementation Plan for Carbon Peaking in Urban and Rural Construction in Xinjiang Uygur Autonomous Region

Source: Compiled by the author.

Table A2: Measures of the Green Development Fund in Some Provinces and Cities

Year	Area	Fund Name	Fund Contents
2020	Nanning City	Guangxi Green Emerging Industries Fund	With a funding scale of CNY5 billion, we will build a high-end green furniture industry chain development pattern.
2020	Liaoning Province	Low-carbon green industry investment fund	With a capital scale of CNY3 billion, the investment will focus on equity investments in outstanding companies in the environmental protection industry and key environmental protection projects.
2020	Lishui City	High-quality green development industry fund	The fund, totaling CNY6 billion, will be invested in five major clusters, including precision manufacturing and healthcare, as well as key industries such as environmental protection and tourism.
2020	Lanzhou	Green Fund	The fund, totaling CNY3 billion, will be invested in key areas of green development, including green chemicals, modern agriculture, and biomedicine.
2021	Ya'an City	Ya'an Green Industry Equity Investment Fund of Funds	The fund has a scale of CNY1 billion and will mainly invest in green industries and other emerging industries.
2021	Chongqing	Guangyang Island Green Development Fund	With a funding scale of CNY3 billion, the project aims to attract talent, technology, and projects to the Eco-City, empowering green and innovative development.
2023	Weihai City	Shandong Green Development Fund Weihai Parallel Fund	Fund size CNY1 billion.
2023	Panzhihua City	Green and Low-Carbon Industry Fund	With a funding scale of CNY3 billion, the funds will focus on investing in strategic emerging and high-end growth industries such as new energy, new materials, modern manufacturing, and cultural tourism.

CNY = renminbi.

Source: Compiled by the author.

Table A3: Forecast of the People's Republic of China Gross Domestic Product Growth Rate

Year	People's Republic of China Gross Domestic Product Growth Rate (%)
2024	5.0
2025	4.6
2026	4.3
2027	4.0
2028–2030	3.6
2031–2035	3.0
2036–2040	2.3
2041–2045	1.8
2045	1.8
2046–2050	1.2
2051–2060	0.5

Source: Macroeconomic and Green Finance Laboratory Research Group, National School of Development, Peking University.

Table A4: Forecast of the People's Republic of China's Population Growth Rate

Year	People's Republic of China's Population Growth Rate (%)
2024	(0.22)
2025	(0.23)
2026	(0.22)
2027	(0.24)
2028	(0.26)
2029	(0.29)
2030	(0.30)
2031	(0.33)
2032	(0.35)
2033	(0.37)
2034	(0.39)
2035	(0.41)
2036	(0.42)
2037	(0.44)
2038	(0.46)
2039	(0.48)
2040	(0.50)
2041	(0.52)
2042	(0.54)
2043	(0.56)
2044	(0.59)
2045	(0.62)
2046	(0.66)
2047	(0.69)
2048	(0.73)
2049	(0.78)
2050	(0.82)
2051	(0.87)
2052	(0.92)
2053	(0.97)
2054	(1.01)
2055	(1.06)
2056	(1.10)
2057	(1.14)
2058	(1.17)
2059	(1.20)
2060	(1.23)

( ) = negative.

Source: United Nations Population Division Data Portal (accessed January 2026).

References

M. Andersson, C. Baccianti, and J. Morgan. 2020. Climate Change and the Macro Economy (No. 243). *ECB Occasional Paper*.

Anhui Provincial People's Government. 2023. Notice on Issuing the Implementation Plan for Carbon Peaking in Anhui Province (Wan Zheng [2022] No. 83). Anhui Provincial People's Government Website. 16 January.

M. Baur, P. A. Bruchez, and S. Nicol. 2021. *Climate Change and Long-term Fiscal Sustainability*. Scoping Paper. Organization for Economic Co-operation and Development, Directorate for Public Governance.

Beijing Municipal People's Government. 2022. Notice on Issuing the "Beijing Carbon Peak Implementation Plan" (Beijing Municipal Government Document No. 31 [2022]). Beijing Municipal People's Government Website. 13 October.

M. S. Black et al. 2024. *Fiscal Implications of Global Decarbonization*. International Monetary Fund.

G. Cayol et al. 2025. *Global Carbon Accounts 2025: Carbon Pricing Instruments and the Unlocked Potential of Carbon Revenues*.

China Academy of Information and Communications Technology (CAICT). 2024. Global Digital Economy White Paper (2023). 26 March.

CAICT. 2024. *Research Report on the Development of China Digital Economy (2025)*. 27 August.

China Finance. 2024. Jiangsu: Implementing the "Dual Carbon" Strategy to Fully Promote Green Development [J]. 2024(23). pp. 28–31. ()

S. Chen, B. Wang, L. Dai. 2025. Constructing a fiscal and tax system adapted to the "dual carbon" goals [J]. *Taxation Research*. 2025(07). pp. 12–19.

Chongqing Municipal Committee of the Communist Party of China and the Chongqing Municipal People's Government. 2022. Implementation Opinions on Fully and Accurately Implementing the New Development Concept and Doing a Good Job in Carbon Peaking and Carbon Neutrality. Chongqing Municipal People's Government Website. 29 July.

Council of the European Union. 2022. Council Approves 2021 Climate Finance Figure. Press release. 28 October.

Daily Economic News. 2022. Xie Zhenhua: The PRC needs over CNY130 trillion in investment to achieve its "dual carbon" goals; green and low-carbon transformation and innovation will create a huge green market. Daily Economic News Website. 2 September.

Economic Daily. 2024. Modern Transportation Moves Towards Intelligent and Green Development. Central Government Portal. 2 September.

European Union. 2021. Proposal for a Regulation of the European Parliament and of the Council Establishing A Carbon Border Adjustment Mechanism. 14 July.

J. Fouré et al. 2023. Public Finance Resilience in the Transition towards Carbon Neutrality: Modeling Policy Instruments in A Global Net-zero Emissions. *OECD Environment Working Papers* No. 214.

Fujian Provincial Committee of the Communist Party of China and the Fujian Provincial People's Government. 2022. Issued the "Implementation Opinions on Fully and Accurately Implementing the New Development Concept and Doing a Good Job in Carbon Peaking and Carbon Neutrality". Fujian Provincial People's Government Website. 21 August.

Gansu Provincial People's Government. 2023. Notice on Issuing the Implementation Plan for Carbon Peak Targeting in Gansu Province (Ganzhengfa [2022] No. 40). Gansu Provincial People's Government Website. 11 May.

General for Taxation and Customs Union of the European Commission. 2017. Fair Taxation of the Digital Economy.

H. Gong. 2021. The practical progress of digital service tax and the controversies and reflections it has caused [J]. *Taxation Research*. 2021(01). pp. 39–46.

Government of the People's Republic of China, Central Committee of the Communist Party of China and State Council. 2021. Opinions on Fully, Accurately and Comprehensively Implementing the New Development Philosophy and Doing a Good Job in Carbon Peaking and Carbon Neutrality. Central Government Website. 24 October.

Government of the People's Republic of China, China Finance Yearbook Editorial Committee. Fiscal Yearbook 2010–2023. China State Finance Magazine Agency.

Government of the People's Republic of China, the CPC Central Committee and the State Council. 2025. Opinions on Promoting Green and Low-Carbon Transformation and Strengthening the Construction of the National Carbon Market. Central Government Website. 24 May.

Government of the People's Republic of China, Ministry of Agriculture and Rural Affairs, National Development and Reform Commission, Ministry of Science and Technology, Ministry of Natural Resources, Ministry of Ecology and Environment, National Forestry and Grassland Administration. 2021. Notice on Issuing the "14th Five-Year Plan for National Agricultural Green Development" (Agricultural Regulation Document [2021] No. 8). Ministry of Agriculture and Rural Affairs Website. 7 September.

Government of the People's Republic of China, Ministry of Agriculture and Rural Affairs, National Development and Reform Commission. 2022. Notice on Issuing the "Implementation Plan for Emission Reduction and Carbon Sequestration in Agriculture and Rural Areas" (Agricultural Science and Education Development [2022] No. 2). Ministry of Agriculture and Rural Affairs Website. 29 June.

Government of the People's Republic of China, Ministry, Center for Urban and Small-Town Reform and Development. 2025. Accurately and Promptly Grasp New Trends in the Urbanization Process and Solidly Promote High-quality Development of New Urbanization. National Development and Reform Commission Website. 7 July.

Government of the People's Republic of China, Ministry of Ecology and Environment. 2024. The People's Republic of China First Biennial Transparency Report on Climate Change. United Nations Framework Convention on Climate Change. December.

Government of the People's Republic of China, Ministry of Finance. 2022. Notice on Issuing the "Opinions on Fiscal Support for Achieving Carbon Peak and Carbon Neutrality" (Cai Zi Huan [2022] No. 53). Central Government Website. 25 May.

Government of the People's Republic of China, Ministry of Finance. 2023. Notice on Amending the "Interim Measures for the Management of Energy Conservation and Emission Reduction Subsidy Funds" (Cai Jian [2023] No. 58). Central Government Website. 7 April.

Government of the People's Republic of China, Ministry of Finance. 2024. Notice on Issuing the "Administrative Measures for Key Ecological Protection, Restoration and Governance Funds" (Cai Zi Huan [2024] No. 6). Ministry of Finance Service Platform for National People's Congress Deputies and National Committee of the Chinese People's Political Consultative Conference. 21 February.

Government of the People's Republic of China, Ministry of Finance. 2025. Report on the Implementation of the PRC's Fiscal Policy in 2024. Central Government Website. 26 March.

Government of the People's Republic of China, Ministry of Finance State Taxation Administration. 2021. Announcement on Improving the Value-Added Tax Policy for Comprehensive Utilization of Resources (Ministry of Finance) State Taxation Administration Announcement No. 40 of 2021. Ministry of Finance Website. 30 December.

Government of the People's Republic of China, Ministry of Finance State Taxation Administration National Development and Reform Commission Ministry of Ecology and Environment. 2021. Announcement on the Publication of the "Catalogue of Enterprise Income Tax Incentives for Environmental Protection, Energy Conservation and Water Conservation Projects (2021 Edition)" and the "Catalogue of Enterprise Income Tax Incentives for Comprehensive Resource Utilization (2021 Edition)" (Ministry of Finance) State Taxation Administration National Development and Reform Commission Ministry of Ecology and Environment Announcement No. 36 of 2021. Ministry of Finance Website. 16 December.

Government of the People's Republic of China, Ministry of Housing and Urban–Rural Development. 2022. Notice on Issuing the "14th Five-Year Plan" for Building Energy Conservation and Green Building Development (Jianbiao [2022] No. 24). Central Government Website. 1 March.

Government of the People's Republic of China, Ministry of Housing and Urban–Rural Development National Development and Reform Commission. 2022. Notice on Issuing the Implementation Plan for Carbon Peaking in Urban and Rural Construction (Jianbiao [2022] No. 53). Central Government Website. 30 June.

Government of the People's Republic of China, Ministry of Industry and Information Technology National Development and Reform Commission Ministry of Ecology and Environment. 2022. Notice on Issuing the Implementation Plan for Carbon Peaking in the Industrial Sector (MIIT Joint Circular [2022] No. 88). Central Government Website. 7 July.

Government of the People's Republic of China, Ministry of Transport. 2021. Notice on Issuing the "14th Five-Year Plan for Green Transportation Development" (Jiaoguifa [2021] No. 104). Central Government Website. 29 October.

Government of the People's Republic of China, Ministry of Transport and nine other departments. 2025. Guiding Opinions on Promoting the Integrated Development of Transportation and Energy (Jiaoguihua Fa [2025] No. 42). Central Government Website. 26 March.

Government of the People's Republic of China, National Development and Reform Commission (NDRC), National Energy Administration. 2022. Notice from the General Office of the State Council on Forwarding the Implementation Plan of the National Development and Reform Commission and the National Energy Administration on Promoting High-Quality Development of New Energy in the New Era (Guo Ban Han [2022] No. 39). Central Government Portal. 30 May.

Government of the People's Republic of China, NDRC, National Energy Administration, National Data Administration. 2024. Notice on Issuing the "Action Plan for Accelerating the Construction of a New Power System (2024–2027)" (Fagai Nengyuan [2024] No. 1128). Central Government Website. 25 July.

Government of the People's Republic of China, NDRC, Ministry of Housing and Urban–Rural Development. 2024. Notice from the General Office of the State Council on Forwarding the "Work Plan for Accelerating Energy Conservation and Carbon Reduction in the Construction Sector" issued by the National Development and Reform Commission and the Ministry of Housing and Urban-Rural Development (Guo Ban Han [2024] No. 20). Central Government Portal. 15 March.

Government of the People's Republic of China NDRC. 2024. Notice of the National Development and Reform Commission on Issuing the "Administrative Measures for Special Investments in Energy Conservation and Carbon Reduction from the Central Budget" (NDRC Circular [2024] No. 338). NDRC Website. 19 September.

Government of the People's Republic of China, National Energy Administration. 2022. Notice on Issuing the "Action Plan for Improving Standardization of Energy Carbon Peaking and Carbon Neutrality". National Energy Administration Website. 9 October.

Government of the People's Republic of China, State Council. 2021. Notice on Issuing the Action Plan for Achieving Carbon Peak Before 2030 (Guofa [2021] No. 23). Central Government Website. 24 October.

Government of the People's Republic of China, State Council. 2024. Notice on Issuing the "Work Plan for Accelerating the Construction of a Dual Control System for Carbon Emissions" (General Office of the State Council Document No. 39 [2024]). Central Government Website. 2 August.

Government of the United Kingdom, Office for Budget Responsibility. 2024. *Fiscal Risk Report*. September.

Green Finance Committee of the China Society for Finance and Banking. 2021. Release of the full text of its report, Research on the Green Finance Roadmap under the Vision of Carbon Neutrality. The report is available on the Green Finance Committee website of the China Society for Finance and Banking. 3 December.

Guangdong Provincial People's Government. 2022. Notice on Issuing the Implementation Plan for Carbon Peaking in Guangdong Province (Yuefu [2022] No. 56). Guangdong Provincial People's Government Website. 23 June.

Guangxi Zhuang Autonomous Region Department of Industry and Information Technology, Guangxi Zhuang Autonomous Region Development and Reform Commission, Guangxi Zhuang Autonomous Region Department of Ecology and Environment. 2023. Notice on Issuing the Implementation Plan for Carbon Peaking in the Industrial Sector of Guangxi Zhuang Autonomous Region (Gui Gongxin Nengyuan [2023] No. 685). Guangxi Zhuang Autonomous Region Department of Industry and Information Technology Website. 3 November.

Guizhou Provincial Committee of the Communist Party of China and Guizhou Provincial People's Government. 2022. Notice on Issuing the "Implementation Plan for Carbon Peaking in Guizhou Province" (Qian Dang Fa [2022] No. 24). Guizhou Provincial People's Government Website. 4 November.

Hainan Provincial People's Government. 2022. Notice on Issuing the Implementation Plan for Carbon Peaking in Hainan Province (Qiongfu [2022] No. 27). Hainan Provincial Development and Reform Commission website. 24 August.

X. Hao. 2025. Reflections on Tax System Reform to Promote Comprehensive Green Transformation [J]. *Fiscal Science*. 2025(01). pp. 91–101.

Hebei Provincial People's Government. 2022. Notice on Issuing the Implementation Plan for Carbon Peaking in Hebei Province (Ji Zheng Fa [2022] No. 3). Hebei Provincial Department of Housing and Urban-Rural Development Website. 19 June.

Heilongjiang Daily. 2022. Implementation Plan for Carbon Peak Achievement in Heilongjiang Province Released. Heilongjiang Provincial People's Government Website. 5 September.

Henan Provincial Committee of the Communist Party of China and Henan Provincial People's Government. 2023. Issued the "Implementation Plan for Carbon Peaking in Henan Province". Henan Provincial People's Government Website. 6 February.

T. Hirsch et al. 2023. New Sources for Public Climate Finance and for the Loss and Damage Fund. Climate Action Network (CAN) Europe.

X. Hong, X. Lin, L. Chen. 2023. A Study on the Effect of Local Green Credit Interest Subsidy Policy—Based on the Perspective of Coordination of Fiscal and Financial Policies [J]. *China Industrial Economics*. 2023(09). pp. 80–97.

L. Huang, S. Yang, and Y. Zhang. 2025. International exploration, controversy and implications of digital service tax [J]. *Taxation and Economic Research*. 30(03). pp. 68–74.

Hunan Provincial People's Government. 2022. Notice on Issuing the "Implementation Plan for Carbon Peaking in Hunan Province" (Xiangzhengfa [2022] No. 19). Hunan Provincial People's Government Website. 15 November.

Hurun Research Institute. 2025. 2024 Hurun Wealth Report. Hurun Rich List Portal. 27 February.

Inner Mongolia Autonomous Region Party Committee, the People's Government of Inner Mongolia Autonomous Region. 2022. Issued the "Implementation Plan for Carbon Peaking in Inner Mongolia Autonomous Region". Website of the Department of Industry and Information Technology of Inner Mongolia Autonomous Region. 19 November.

Institute for Climate Economics. 2025. Global Carbon Accounts 2025 (accessed January 2026).

International Monetary Fund. 2023. *Climate Crossroads: Fiscal Policies in a Warming World*.

N. Jiang and S. Chen. 2023. Research on Green Fiscal Expenditure Policy under the "dual carbon" goals [J]. *New Finance (Government Finance)*. 2023(12). pp. 28–29.

Jiangsu Provincial Committee of the Communist Party of China and Jiangsu Provincial People's Government. 2022. Notice on Issuing the Implementation Opinions on Promoting High-Quality Development and Doing a Good Job in Carbon Peaking and Carbon Neutrality. Jiangsu Provincial People's Government Website. 30 January.

Jiangxi Provincial People's Government (2022). Notice on Issuing the Implementation Plan for Carbon Peaking in Jiangxi Province. Jiangxi Provincial Development and Reform Commission Website. 18 July.

Jilin Provincial People's Government. 2022. Notice on Issuing the Implementation Plan for Carbon Peaking in Jilin Province (Jilin Government Document No. 11 [2022]). Jilin Provincial Government of the People's Republic of China, People's Government Website. 22 July.

J. Li et al. 2015. Report on the Development of People's Livelihood in The PRC [M]. Peking University Press. 201511(216).

M. Liao. 2024. Give full play to the fiscal function to promote green and low-carbon development [J]. *China Finance*. 2024(23): p. 1.

Liaoning Provincial Department of Housing and Urban-Rural Development, Liaoning Provincial Development and Reform Commission. 2023. Notice on Issuing the "Implementation Plan for Carbon Peaking in Urban and Rural Construction in Liaoning Province" (Liaoning Housing and Construction [2023] No. 45). Liaoning Provincial People's Government Website. 30 June.

H. Ma and J. He. 2022. Reflections on how government green procurement systems can help achieve "dual carbon" goals. *The PRC Government Procurement News*. 25 July.

H. Ma and F. Wang. 2021. Reflections on The PRC's Tax System Structure during the 14th Five-Year Plan Period [J]. *Research on Financial and Economic Issues*. 2021(11). pp. 88–98.

Network for Greening the Financial System. 2023. *Scaling Up Blended Finance for Climate Mitigation and Adaptation in Emerging Market and Developing Economies (EMDEs)*.

Ningxia Hui Autonomous Region Party Committee People's Government. 2022. Notice on Issuing the "Implementation Plan for Carbon Peaking in Ningxia Hui Autonomous Region". Ningxia Hui Autonomous Region Development and Reform Commission Website. 25 October.

Oil Change International. 2023. Open Letter: Global North leaders Must Redirect Trillions from Fossils, Debt, and the 1% to Address Global Crises. 19 June.

Oil Change International. 2025. *Paying for Climate Chaos: US Federal Subsidies for Fossil Fuel Production*.

Organisation for Economic Co-operation and Development (OECD), International Monetary Fund, Germany, Indonesia, United States, et al. 2016. The PRC's Efforts to Phase Out and Rationalize Inefficient Fossil Fuel Subsidies: G20 Peer Review Report. OECD.

T. Ouyang and J. Xu. 2024. Institutional prospects for promoting digital tax legislation under the dual circulation pattern [J]. *Journal of the National Tax Administration Cadre Academy*. 37(06). pp. 37–46.

D. Pan, C. Chen, and M. Grubb. 2021. Financial Policy and Low-Carbon Economic Transition: A Study Based on Growth Perspective [J]. *Financial Research*. 2021(12). pp. 1–19.

X. Pang. 2024. Functional Analysis, Progress and Policy Recommendations of The PRC's Carbon Finance Market. Central University of Finance and Economics International Institute of Green Finance website. 2 April.

People's Bank of China. 2021. Governor Yi Gang attended and addressed the high-level seminar on Green Finance and Climate Policy jointly held by the People's Bank of the PRC and the International Monetary Fund. People's Bank of China website. 15 April.

People's Daily Overseas Edition. 2023. Developing New Power Systems to Support the "Dual Carbon" Goal. Belt and Road Energy Cooperation Portal. 19 June.

Policy Research Center for Environment and Economy and Environmental Defense Fund. 2023. *The PRC's Policies and Actions on Carbon Peaking and Carbon Neutrality*.

S. Qi and S. Cheng. 2024. Experiences, achievements, challenges and policy considerations in the construction of the PRC's carbon market [J]. *International Economic Review*. 2024(03). pp. 108–128.

Qinghai Provincial People's Government. 2022. Notice on Issuing the Implementation Plan for Carbon Peak Targeting in Qinghai Province (Qingzheng [2022] No. 65). Qinghai Provincial People's Government Website. 18 December.

Research Group of Macroeconomic and Green Finance Laboratory, National School of Development, Peking University. 2025. Exploring the Establishment of a Funding Support Mechanism for Fair Transition in the PRC—Taking Shanxi Province as a Typical Case.

J. A. Richards, D. Hillman, and L. Boughey. 2019. The Climate Damages Tax: a Guide to What It Is and How It Works. Stamp Out Poverty.

Seghini and Dees. 2024. The Green Transition and Public Finances. *Banque De France Working Papers* No. 949.

Shaanxi Provincial People's Government. 2023. Notice on Issuing the Implementation Plan for Carbon Peaking (Shaanxi Government Document No. 18 [2022]). Shaanxi Provincial People's Government Website. 17 February.

Shandong Provincial People's Government. 2022. Notice on Issuing the Implementation Plan for Carbon Peaking in Shandong Province (Lu Zheng Zi [2022] No. 242). Shandong Provincial Department of Ecology and Environment Website. 29 December.

Shanghai Municipal People's Government. 2022. Notice on Issuing the "Shanghai Carbon Peak Implementation Plan" (Shanghai Municipal Government Document No. 7 [2022]). Shanghai Municipal People's Government Website. 28 July.

Shanxi Provincial People's Government. 2023. Notice on Issuing the Implementation Plan for Carbon Peak Targeting in Shanxi Province (Jin Zheng Fa [2022] No. 29). Shanxi Provincial People's Government Website. 9 January.

Shenzhen Development and Reform Commission. 2023. The second in a series on Shenzhen's innovative business environment pilot projects: Green taxes and fees boost new energy vehicles. At the end of last year, Shenzhen's total number of new energy vehicles exceeded 766,000, ranking among the world's top. Shenzhen Development and Reform Commission website. 24 May.

Sichuan Provincial People's Government. 2023. Notice on Issuing the Implementation Plan for Carbon Peaking in Sichuan Province (Sichuan Government Document No. 37 [2022]). Sichuan Provincial People's Government Website. 5 January.

Tianjin Municipal People's Government. 2022. Notice on Issuing the Implementation Plan for Carbon Peaking in Tianjin (Jin Zheng Fa [2022] No. 18). Tianjin Municipal People's Government Website. 14 September.

Q. Tong, et al. 2022. Analysis of problems and policy recommendations in the operation of the national carbon market [J]. *China Economic and Trade Guide*. 2022(03). pp. 58–59.

Tsinghua University Institute for Climate Change and Sustainable Development. 2020. *Research on the PRC's Long-Term Low-Carbon Development Strategy and Transformation Path*. Tsinghua University Institute for Climate Change and Sustainable Development Portal. 12 October.

B. Wang and Q. Xu. 2021. Reflections on the Trial Implementation of the Consumption Place Taxation Principle for Digital Service Transactions in my country [J]. *Taxation Research*. 2021(12). pp. 55–61.

K. Wang and C. Lü. 2025. *Global and Chinese Carbon Market Review and Outlook (2025)* [R]. Energy and Environmental Policy Research Center, Beijing Institute of Technology. 12 January.

M. Wemaëre, L. Vallejo, and M. Colombier. 2023. *Financing Loss and Damage: Overview of Tax/Levy Instruments Under Discussion*. Institute for Sustainable Development and International Relations.

Y. Xie. 2025. Current Status, Problems and Lessons Learned in the Construction of the PRC's Green Tax System under the Dual Carbon Target [J]. *Economic Circles*. 2025(01): pp. 68–77.

H. Xu and X. Zhang. 2018. Discussion on improving the PRC's green tax system [J]. *Taxation Research*. 2018(9). pp. 101–104.

J. Zhang. 2025. Suggestions for optimizing the green tax system under the "dual carbon" goals [J]. *Market Weekly*. 38(02). pp. 34–37.

S. Zhang. 2022. Integration ideas and specific measures for local government fiscal funds related to ecological civilization construction under the "dual carbon" goals–taking Hebei Province as an example [J]. *Fiscal Science*. 2022(06). pp. 117–126.

Z. Zhou and S. Zhang. 2021. Carbon Neutrality and Green Finance: Guiding Services and Turning Challenges into Opportunities. *CICC Insights*. 22 March.

www.ingramcontent.com/pod-product-compliance
Lightning Source LLC
Chambersburg PA
CBHW041756220926
51847CB00014B/227
* 9 7 8 9 2 9 2 7 7 8 6 3 7 *